More Praise for

The Office Sutras

"With wisdom and humor, Marcia Menter teaches us that spiritual growth needn't be confined to a church, temple, meditation room, or synagogue. We can be connected to our souls anywhere, anytime. Menter offers us the tools needed to turn even the most dreaded of workspaces into a place where our spirits can soar."

—Amanda Ford, author of
Retail Therapy: Life Lessons Learned While Shopping

"Go to work
work hard
get ahead
get a soul
feel great
with the wisdom from Marcia Menter's *The Office Sutras*."
—David Marell, author of *Be Generous*

"Author Marcia Menter raises some provocative questions about ourselves in the workplace and answers them with wit and wisdom and clearly a great breadth of experience. I loved being reminded that welcoming imperfection into our lives is a guide to spiritual practice. I was inspired to look at how much of my true self I brought to work with me each day, a very enlightening task."

—Hailey Klein, author of *The Way of Chang*

The Office Sutras

Exercises for Your Soul

at Work

The Office Sutras

Exercises for Your Soul

at Work

Marcia Menter

Red Wheel
Boston, MA / York Beach, ME

First published in 2003 by Red Wheel/Weiser, LLC
York Beach, ME
With offices at: 368 Congress Street, Boston, MA 02210
www.redwheelweiser.com

Library of Congress Cataloging-in-Publication Data
Menter, Marcia.
  The office sutras : exercises for your soul at work / Marcia Menter.
    p. cm.
    ISBN 1-59003-020-6
1. Work—Moral and ethical aspects. 2. Interpersonal relations.
3. Motivation (Psychology) 4. Self-actualization (Psychology)
5. Employees—Conduct of life. I. Title.
  HD4905.M39 2003
    158.7—dc21

                                                      2003008628

Designed and typeset in Sabon by Joyce C. Weston
Printed in Canada
TCP
10 09 08 07 06 05 04 03
 8 7 6 5 4 3 2 1

To my husband

Contents

Introduction

Me: I've been asked to write a book about spirituality in the workplace.

My friend Jennie: Is it fiction or nonfiction?

Me: With any luck, it'll be nonfiction, and shut up.

Jennie: No, really—what could possibly be spiritual about the average workplace? Is this one of those books where I'm supposed to assume the lotus position at my desk? Because I'm telling you right now, that's not going to happen.

Me: No contortions required, I promise. Though I may suggest an occasional centering breath.

Jennie: That's going to make me feel more spiritual at work? I don't think so. Look, I *like* my job, basically. But it feels completely separate from the spiritual side of my life. I wish I could say I worked to nourish my soul, but I don't. I work because I need the paycheck. And I don't necessarily conduct myself with sweetness and light. In my business, sweet guys finish last. How, exactly, is that supposed to be spiritual?

Me: Well, yes, that's a tough question . . .

Jennie: And *please* don't tell me I'm supposed to find vocational fulfillment by following my bliss, because I know perfectly well I can't make a living following my bliss, and that's a sore point for me. Am I going to finish this book hating my life or feeling happy about it?

Me: Feeling happy, I hope.

Jennie: I hope so, too. This isn't one of those books filled with blank lines for me to write Deep Thoughts in, is it?

Me: I've always wanted to write a book full of blank lines, but no, this isn't it.

Jennie: Well, what kind of book *is* it?

Okay, here's the short answer. Most of us have to work for a living, and most of us work at jobs which are, to put it charitably, imperfect. We're not doing what we once dreamed of doing, assuming we were lucky enough to dream. Instead, we're stuck in jobs that overtax us, underpay us, exhaust us, bore us. We find ourselves having to answer to idiots. We encounter more kinds of frustration than we thought existed.

That's business. It's also life.

The basic premise of this book is that we're on a spiritual
journey every second of our lives, not just during those times we
set aside to contemplate the cosmos. The job you have right now,
no matter how frustrating, no matter how screamingly imperfect, is part of your spiritual path. The work you're doing right
now, no matter how thankless or inane, is noble work, because it
presents you with exactly what you need for your spiritual
growth, *assuming you pay the right kind of attention to it.*

I'm not promising that a job that makes you miserable will
suddenly fulfill you if you apply the ideas in this book. But I
am saying that many keys to vocational happiness lie right in
front of you, in the present moment—not at the end of some
follow your bliss rainbow. This book is designed to help you
find and use those keys, to become deeply aware of your spiritual self at work.

The difficulties we meet on our career paths are spiritual
obstacles as well as temporal ones. Facing these difficulties in
a spirit of self-love and compassion can bring us closer to our
truer, deeper selves. When we remind ourselves that we are
spiritual, worthy beings even in the midst of the most mundane, soul-wearying situations, we sanctify our lives. Working
for a living and walking a spiritual path turn out to be one and
the same thing.

4   The chapters in this book are short, but they'll give you a lot to think about, so I suggest that you read just one at a time—one a day, perhaps. (Though of course you can read them any way, and in any order, you like.) You'll note that there are "keywords" at the opening of each chapter. I've included a digest of these in the back of the book. Consider it a glossary—okay, a cheat sheet—of the basic ideas presented here. Refer to it when you want to be reminded of these ideas without having to reread entire chapters.

One more thing. This book really is nonfiction, but it tells a fascinating story—the story of your soul at work. All I ask you to remember for now is that you're the hero.

Chapter 1

Work as a Spiritual Practice

Look, I believe there's a real need for a book about spirituality and work, if only because I know so many people who regard themselves as spiritual beings at least part of the time, who earn their livings in environments that don't seem spiritual any of the time. My friend Jennie, for example, meditates every morning, or at least thinks about it, before setting off to do battle in an office where the politics are so thick you can't even cut them with a sword, and Jennie's pretty good with a sword. She is by any definition a capable and honorable businesswoman. She wants to increase profits—and beat the competition—by making the best product possible and selling it honestly and aggressively. She wants to create a nurturing work environment where her staff can function at its peak. And she wants to remember the spiritual values that matter most to her and keep them close to her heart. She wants, in other words, to bring her whole self to the office—competitiveness, heart, soul, and all.

Most days, though, she's happy if she can just get through the pile on her desk. There are so many tasks clamoring for her attention she can barely focus on any of them, let alone keep her larger goals in view. Her company, like many these days, dedicates more energy to the bottom line than to the well-being of its employees, so Jennie's department has the kind of budget that fosters an atmosphere of insufficiency. There are never quite enough resources to do the job right. Her office is stuffy; she suspects that no one ever actually dusts it. She usually has a headache by about 4 P.M. And when she gets cranky or frustrated, which happens a lot, she does not recognize herself as the spiritual being on the meditation cushion longing to be her best self. That's when she starts to wonder: Have I taken a wrong turn somewhere? Am I doing this kind of work just because I'm good at it and I need the money? How much of what I'm doing is really meaningful? Am I making a difference? Am I wasting my life?

Jennie claims to like her job, and I believe her. But she feels out of balance because she spends so much of her life at work, putting in the time and effort that will, among other things, reward her with a paycheck that enables her to pay her mortgage and help feed her family. She's working for her living, in other words, and the more she works, the less she feels like she's living.

Here's my question: Is it possible to seek enlightenment—or, if you're lukewarm on enlightenment, to feel alive, whole, useful, and even joyful—in an imperfect job that eats up most of your time and energy and basically requires you to do the same thing over and over? Say you're in a job you don't love, or even a job you hate. Is it possible to function primarily from your spiritual center even then?

I believe it is. But first, it's necessary to be clear in your own mind and heart about what "spirituality" is, and what it's not. Spirituality, at least as I experience it, is not about being a good person all the time, or about feeling connected to God all the time, or even about finding happiness in the sweet by and by. Spirituality is about *spirit,* about the force that moves in you, calls to you, shakes you awake, *right here, right now.* Spirituality is about waking up again and again, about being exactly who you are in the present moment—the present moment being all you have to work with at any given time. And as I'm sure you know, some moments are a whole lot more present than others. Sometimes you're awake, and sometimes you're dead asleep. Sometimes you feel connected to

God—or Spirit, or your spiritual center, or whatever you call your experience of the divine—and sometimes you don't. Sometimes you live up to your best self, and sometimes you fall laughably, humiliatingly short.

There's a good reason why we speak about spiritual *practice*. Spiritually speaking, we're not there yet; we're still practicing. We're working on something we haven't mastered and don't fully understand—seeking the divine, learning compassion, being a good person—and giving it our best shot, over and over.

I don't know what form your spiritual practice takes, but I'm assuming you find the idea congenial if you're reading this book. So think for a moment about the things you do that connect you to your deeper self. When you sit down to pray or meditate, when you dance, climb rocks, or play the piano, when you do anything that takes you to a holy place, you expect to crash head on into your own imperfections. You know you're going to hit wrong notes, or lose track of the meditative breath and think about breakfast instead, or spew utter drivel when you're trying to write the Great American Novel, or cheat on a tough yoga posture, or harbor evil thoughts about someone you wish you could love. You know that a certain amount of failure is inevitable, that any work worth doing is a work in progress.

We all know this. In any endeavor that can remotely be classified as spiritual, we expect to struggle with feelings of unworthiness, despair, terror, or anger, and with our own infuriating slowness to comprehend the obvious. (A sure sign you've uncovered an important truth: It feels like it's been right in front of you all along and you simply haven't seen it.) So we learn to cut ourselves some slack. We hope we'll be able to haul ourselves up toward the next epiphany sooner or later. We believe that some kind of comfort will come, if not now, eventually.

Our spiritual practice is the arena to which we bring every bit of our unfinished, muddled, willful, absurdly arrogant selves. We know we're not supposed to be perfect; imperfection, after all, is what we're here for. Imperfection is the raw material for compassion, transformation, joy. Imperfection is what practice makes perfect.

Right? So how is it that the minute we get to the office—the minute the alarm goes off on weekday mornings—we stop welcoming imperfection and start fighting it? How is it that we refuse to have compassion for our own work-related frustration, our anger, our boredom, our physical exhaustion? Where's that holy place now? Are we saving it for our spiritual practice? Suppose I told you that your office is a holy place, even if you feel a sinking despair every time you walk into it?

You don't have to believe me. Not yet, anyway. All I ask is that you consider the possibility that the job you have right now, for all its imperfections—no, *because* of its imperfections—is just as spiritual as any other part of your life. Maybe more spiritual, because it confronts you with all the stuff you really need to look at: Big Deep Issues of self-worth, fulfillment, and paying your way in the world.

Think for a moment about your workspace. Is there enough light, enough privacy? Does it feel like your personal space? Or like an impersonal territory you're occupying for the duration? Is there anything beautiful about it? Is it supposed to be beautiful? Is it clean and orderly? Cluttered and random? Could you imagine bringing your mother there? Or praying there?

Now think about your salary. Is it enough? If not, how much is enough?

Now think about the job itself, the tasks you're faced with every day. Is there enough pleasure in your work to balance out the inevitable frustrations, at least some of the time?

Express in one word the feeling you get in your gut when you picture your boss.

Think about your friends and colleagues. Do you know someone who's stuck in a job she hates, or who works hours that are too long, takes too few vacations, pushes herself too

hard? Someone who merely goes through the motions of his
job because he's only doing it for the paycheck, and who there-
fore spends at least 40 hours each week deadening his mind
and spirit so he can "really" live outside of work?

Are there regular conversations in your office about how the
people in charge are cheap, clueless, unfair, or unfeeling? Do
you see your colleagues as spiritual beings? Do you think they
see you that way?

Do you bring your whole self to the office? If not, which
parts do you leave at home?

One more question: Can you see your own divinity in the
mundane tasks before you, in the pile of paperwork on your
desk, in your relationships with your colleagues? Well, it's
there, right in front of you.

The purpose of this book is to help you look for your divinity, in ways as practical as playing scales on the piano or count-
ing breaths in meditation. I'm not going to tell you how to
follow your own spiritual path, which after all is different from
mine or anyone else's. I just hope to remind you that you're on
that path every moment of your working life and that your colleagues are, too, whether you ever openly acknowledge it or not.

I also hope to encourage you to think about your job as an
active part of your spiritual practice, an arena that challenges

you spiritually as well as professionally. One basic premise of this book is that the things that drive you craziest at work can be doorways to growth and understanding if you approach them with an open mind and heart. In the following chapters, you'll find exercises (simple! I promise!) to help you do just that. You might find it helpful, if you're so inclined, to share this book with a friend or two, or even form a study group, so you can explore some of these issues together.

Who am I to be talking to you about spirituality and work? Someone who's brought home a lot of paychecks of varying size, who's worked for bad bosses and good, who's sat in endless meetings in windowless offices wondering what the hell she was supposed to be doing with her life. Someone who has enjoyed her job, sometimes. Someone who has loved and been loved by her colleagues, sometimes (but not always). Someone who once programmed her office screensaver to read, "What does not kill me makes me stronger." Someone who prays a lot, and who believes that prayers are generally answered, though the answers often seem to come out of left field.

In a recent study at Stanford University, high-level professional women were asked what factors had most contributed to their success in life. The thing they cited most frequently was love—the love and support of the people around them. Next came drive and determination—their own desire to create success for themselves. And the third most frequently cited factor was spirituality. Not financial backing, not education, not networking, but some manner of spiritual belief to guide them through good times and bad. The fact that so many respondents volunteered that spirituality was important to them came as a surprise to the psychologist, Laraine Zappert, Ph.D., who conducted the study. After all, as Dr. Zappert pointed out to me, there aren't many obvious spiritual role models in the top echelons of business.

There are, however, growing numbers of business people who openly seek to express their spiritual values in their work. At this writing, more and more companies are exploring, or thinking about exploring, ways to acknowledge their employees' spiritual lives. This is a tricky proposition in a society that honors individual freedom; obviously, there's no legal or logical way to mandate spirituality as a company policy. But individual executives, even chief executives, can bring their spiritual and moral values to bear on their jobs. And individual employees at every level can change their workplace cultures for the better by the simple, sacred act of remembering that they are, in fact, spiritual beings.

And you, sitting at your desk, or standing behind your

counter, or traveling to your next appointment, can remember to tell yourself: This is my path, and there are no wrong turns on it. There is only the next step, and whatever it is, I can bring a blessing to it.

Mantra for the Bad Days:

I might as well bring my whole soul to work.

After all, that's where I need it most.

Chapter 2 What Feels Like Work

········ KEYWORDS ········
work ■ resistance

I don't know about you, but I've always wanted to find work I could love. Happiness in work, after all, is right up there with happiness in love as one of the big things we strive for as human beings. But work, as a literal, necessary fact of our lives, has nothing to do with happiness. It has to do with getting stuff done.

Frank Gaynor's *Concise Dictionary of Science* defines work as "the result of force acting against resistance to produce motion in a body." The dictionary goes on, laconically, to say, "It should be noted that the element of time does not come into consideration concerning work. If a weight of 50 pounds is raised 20 feet, 1000 foot-pounds of work have been accomplished. Whether it required a few minutes or several weeks to raise the weight makes no difference."

There you have it, folks. Work equals force acting against

resistance within an infinitely expandable time frame. If I have a project to finish and I don't feel like doing it, I can put it off indefinitely, causing myself infinite agita in the process, but the work still remains to be done. So there are two parts to every task that feels like work: doing the task itself, and overcoming our own resistance to it. The greater the resistance, the more enormous the task.

No matter where you look it up, "work" is not a fun word. According to Webster's dictionary, work is the "sustained physical or mental effort to overcome obstacles and achieve an objective . . . the labor, task, or duty that is one's accustomed means of livelihood . . . an activity in which one exerts strength." Obstacles and effort and duty and exertion. Nowhere is it written that we're supposed to enjoy any of this. We all wish work could be fun, and sometimes it even is. But most of the time, work is the thing staring us in the face that we'd rather not do right now but that has to be done sooner or later: diving into the dreaded pile of papers on your desk; writing the report; having the tricky conversation with the annoying colleague or the difficult client.

Being at work involves, to some degree, being in a chronic state of resistance to some aspect of your job. Think about how you feel on Sunday nights, even if you basically like your job: It's that old school-night feeling. You're coming to the end of your free weekend time, which hasn't been long enough, and tomorrow morning you have to get up and go to the office. Do you draw a demarcation right there, between the time you dedicate to making a living and the time you get to spend on yourself and your family? Between the things you have to do and the things you want to do?

Work is the stuff you have to do whether you want to or not. Even if you have the ideal job, you're going to resent having to do parts of it sometimes. Believe it or not, this is a *good* thing. The resentments, the parts of your life that chafe, are the things that need your attention, the things that help keep you awake. This is as true of your personal spiritual path as it is of your day job.

That's why I'm not going to tell you that the more spiritually evolved you are, the more you're going to love your job. There are any number of self-help gurus out there who propagate what I call the Follow Your Bliss Myth, the idea that if you are truly connected to your spiritual center, you'll be able to do the thing you love for a living and be heaped with the abundance of the universe. (My personal reaction to the notion of being heaped with abundance is to duck, but maybe that's just me.) Of course, this myth has a core of truth; that's why it's so enticing. It really is true that the more you're connected to your spiritual center, the more you'll know what kinds of activities make you happy, and the more time and energy you'll devote to those activities. It's also true that as you go along on your path, you'll find ways to do more of the things that make you happy and fewer of the things that don't. And yes, you might even find that your passion for baking gingerbread men can burgeon into a vast gingerbread empire. I wish you the best, I really do. I just want to make the point that your degree of job satisfaction is not a measure of your spirituality.

You can be a deeply spiritual person and hate your job. You can be on the "right" path and hate your job. You can be evolved as all get out and curse the moment the alarm goes off on Monday mornings.

Work equals force acting against resistance. And work is what we're here for. On a brute physical level, we have to tame our environment to survive—to create shelter for our furless bodies, to coax nourishment from the recalcitrant earth, to find water we can drink and wash in. In the modern world, in a place like, say, Passaic, New Jersey, our bodily raiment comes from The Gap and our nourishment comes from the Stop & Shop, but we still have to find some way to pay for it all. We also have to pay for the things that nourish our souls—our music systems and yoga classes and vacations and, oh, right, whatever our kids need to nourish *their* bodies and souls. If you are gainfully employed, if you are making ends meet and even doing a little better than that, you're already accomplishing quite a lot, spiritually speaking. You're paying your way. Please take a good long moment to pat yourself on the back for this. It's not easy.

Work is what we're here for. Not just the work of supporting ourselves, but the work of transforming ourselves. As spiritual beings, we're here to take the stuff of our lives—our physical, emotional, and mental endowment—and produce motion in it, against resistance and over time. We're here to become better, freer, happier, more loving human beings, and to give something of ourselves back to the world. Our raw materials for this work are our discontents, our imperfect jobs, our unfinished lives—everything that's right in front of us, the very stuff we don't want to face. So work can, ultimately, make us happy, but it's still, well, *work*.

I know a young woman named Madeleine who works for a small public relations firm. One of her least favorite tasks is calling reporters and pitching stories about her firm's clients—an important part of her job, since her firm is paid to get its clients covered by the media. She likes coming up with the story ideas themselves because she thinks of this as the creative aspect of her job. But she hates the drudgery of calling reporters, getting their voice mail, calling them back, and (usually) hearing them say no once she finally reaches them. She hates this task because it feels useless to her—most of the reporters are too busy to listen to a pitch, but she has to be able to tell the client she's called them in order to justify her firm's fee. She also hates having to ask anybody for anything, and she especially hates being rejected over and over again.

On days when she has a lot of calls to make, Madeleine goes through an elaborate procrastination ritual. She makes a list of the people she needs to call, decides she needs a cup of coffee, finds the pot empty, makes a fresh pot (muttering that she's somehow the one who always ends up on kitchen duty and it isn't fair), decides she needs to go to the ladies room, engages a similarly procrastinating colleague in a long conversation en route to the ladies room and, if she's clever, gets down to her calls just as most of the people on her list are going to lunch. Ah—lunchtime.

There are days when Madeleine looks at her list and sees the ruin of a promising young mind: This cannot, cannot be what she hoped and dreamed and went to school for. There are days when she finds a way to jolly herself through the task, joking with colleagues about how ridiculous it is. And there are days when she actually comes close to enjoying it, when she has a conversation with a reporter that makes her feel like she knows what she's doing.

As you have probably observed by now, Madeleine is in the wrong job. People who hate pitching reporters probably shouldn't be publicists. But Madeleine is just starting her professional life. She's still figuring out who she is and what she wants to do. She hasn't yet realized that calling reporters is basically a sales function and that she's not a salesperson in her soul. All she knows is that she'll do practically anything to avoid picking up that phone.

Sooner or later, Madeleine may work out a way to rid herself of this task. Maybe she'll buckle down and get herself promoted so she can delegate the callbacks to someone else and concentrate on the stuff she likes. Maybe she'll get utterly fed up with publicity and start looking for a job in another field. Or maybe she'll get fired—a distinct possibility given her track record—and realize she really wanted to be a reporter all along. My point is that Madeleine's resistance is trying to tell her something, and the sooner she starts listening to it, the sooner she'll be able to move through it.

If she doesn't move through her resistance, she'll probably

spend a certain amount of time mired in it. She'll have long "I hate my job" conversations with friends, and expend untold energy reminding herself that she "should" be on the phone making those calls. She may even fall into despair about not knowing what she wants to do with her life. Resistance can be very seductive. As long as you're stuck in it, you don't have to actually do anything other than be unhappy.

But there's a way to work through even the stickiest resistance. It begins with seeing your resistance for what it is, naming it, taking its measure. The minute you do this, you've taken your first step out of the mire. You've begun to work.

· ·
Exercise: Noticing Your Resistance

It's counterproductive, not to mention self-punishing, to try to force your way through your resistance to a task. Forcing yourself to do something you hate doesn't make you nobler, just unhappier. The best method for overcoming your own resistance is to apply a little consciousness to it.

Think of an aspect of your job that really feels like work to you—a task or project you'd go to any lengths to avoid. Try to choose a smallish, specific task rather than something global like, say, getting up in the morning. The more specific the task, the more easily you'll be able to focus on it. If you tell yourself you hate your whole job, you're just inviting yourself to wallow in your resistance.

Imagine yourself sitting down to this task, with a deadline looming. How do you feel? Don't analyze. Just observe: How does your resistance feel in your body? Is there a tightness in your chest? A gnawing in the pit of your stomach? Do you feel like running away? Or do you feel suddenly tired, as though you want to collapse?

I'm betting this feeling, whatever form it takes, is a familiar one. Take a little time to observe it *without thinking about it.* If you think anything at all, think, "This is what my resistance feels like." If you find this sentence simplistic, let me remind you that it's already a radically different thought from "I hate this job" or "Don't make me do this" or "I'm so tired."

If you simply notice your resistance whenever it arises, you'll have accomplished a lot. For one thing, you'll have established yourself as the observer of your resistance instead of the unfortunate drone who's mired in it. For another thing, you'll begin to pick up patterns—to see, for example, whether certain kinds of tasks always set off this feeling, or whether certain conditions (the person who sets the task, the deadline, the time of day) are triggers.

You can also, over time, begin to notice the emotional content of your resistance. Is it singing a song you've sung before? Are you (for example) angry at someone or something? Is this an anger you've felt before in your life? When? Are you angry at the idea of being told what to do, even if no one's actually telling you what to do?

Does some aspect of the task feel daunting, causing you to fear you'll fail or not measure up in some way? When have you felt this fear before? Can you imagine doing the task without the fear?

Or are you possibly bored out of your mind and body? Are you longing for something completely different without letting yourself know it? Do you believe it's even possible to do something completely different with your life? Well, why not?

....

You see what I mean: Noticing your resistance is a radical and dynamic act, because it means noticing the feelings and issues that lie beneath that resistance. I'm not saying you're supposed to notice your resistance, plumb your deepest emotions and motivations, and change your life before five o'clock this afternoon. Remember what the *Concise Dictionary of Science* says: "The element of time does not come into consideration concerning work." You have a whole lifetime to accomplish the work of being alive. You may as well start with seeing how you feel about the task in front of you, especially if it's a task you'd rather not do.

Mantra for the Bad Days:

I'm working harder than I think. I'm accomplishing more than I know. And right now, I'm going to give myself points for just showing up.

Chapter 3

Are They Paying Me Enough?

One benefit of having worked at more than one top woman's magazine is that I know what it feels like to walk away from a glamour job. I've worked with people who had seven-figure incomes. I've even, briefly, had a six-figure income myself. I've taken limousines (much overrated) and been sent on business trips to Paris (every bit as wonderful as it's cracked up to be). I've worn designer clothing (badly) and eaten in top restaurants (extremely well). So I can tell you what you lose when you leave a sexy job with outrageous perks: Not much.

I'm not saying it hasn't been fun, or that I haven't done my share of rewarding work along the way. I'm just saying that as an end in itself, glamour is pretty meaningless and surprisingly easy to walk away from, at least for me. Money . . . now, money is nice. But it, too, is meaningless as an end in itself. Assuming you're making enough money to meet your needs—a major assumption, granted—having more and more money does not make you feel more and more fulfilled. It does, however, make you richer, and I'm not about to knock that. Money can buy you freedom, and freedom is a good thing.

The question I'd like you to ask yourself—and not try to answer just yet—is: How much money do I really need to make? How much is Enough? How will I know when I'm making Enough?

You probably don't share your salary history with many people. Most of us don't. We regard our paychecks as private things. We tend to feel, though we know better, that our salaries somehow measure our success as human beings, our ability to pay our way in life. But any gainfully employed person knows that there is no rhyme, reason, or justice to the way salaries are handed out in the working world. Companies pay whatever they can get away with paying. If you leave a job because it isn't paying you enough, your employer may have to fork over a higher salary to attract a replacement. This doesn't mean your replacement is any better at the job than you were, it just means the person they wanted was more expensive than you. What makes an employee more expensive? Beats me. I've seen truly incompetent people who manage to rake in higher and higher salaries and truly talented people whose incomes never amount to much. So have you, I'm sure.

Then, too, some careers are much more lucrative than others. I know an investment banker who at age 30 is making more money than he has a clue how to spend; he's already redone his Tribeca loft twice. I also know a concert pianist who at age 65 isn't sure where his next month's rent is coming from. Both men love their work with pure hearts and devote endless hours to it. But it's hard for the pianist to be scraping by after a lifetime's dedication to his art. It makes him feel the world doesn't value his talent, and this makes him very tired. He has come to equate making money with selling out; he wears his poverty like a badge of honor. The investment banker, on the other hand, equates money with success. He has no trouble believing he's earning every penny of his enormous income, even though it could support a small Third World country. So both men, in different ways, view their incomes as expressions of their self-worth. You can't earn a pittance, or a fortune, and not have your self-image be affected by it.

Everyone who brings home a paycheck grapples with the slippery relationship between salary and self-worth. When we accept a job, we agree to barter our time, intelligence, experience, and energy for a certain amount of money, security, satisfaction, and possibly prestige. Some of these things are intangibles, but time, energy, and money are about as tangible as you can get. After a long, trying day or a long, trying week, it's natural to start wondering whether the time and energy we're putting in is worth the money we're taking out. We ask ourselves: Am I being paid what I'm worth? Would I be happier in a less fulfilling but more lucrative career, or vice versa? Is this the way I really want to be spending my life?

If we're supporting a family, the questions get even trickier: Shouldn't my family's needs come first, before my level of personal satisfaction with my work? But if I'm only working for the money, won't my family feel my lack of fulfillment and be affected by it? Does personal fulfillment even enter the picture when other people are dependent on my income?

There's no easy answer to questions like these. You can kick the money-changers out of your temple, whatever sort of temple it may be, but you still need money to live. Figuring out how much money you need is a spiritual exercise in itself.

What is the spiritually correct approach to making money, anyhow? Judging by what I've seen in self-help books and the media, there seem to be two basic views on the matter, and both are pretty simplistic. The first, which I call the Create Your Own Abundance approach, involves the idea that money is an expression of the abundance of the universe, and as spiritually evolved beings, we need and deserve that abundance. If we can just visualize what we want really clearly, abundance will be showered upon us because, hey, we create our own reality. If abundance doesn't materialize, it's because we screwed up somehow. We didn't visualize clearly enough. We didn't Follow Our Bliss. Or we don't, in our hearts, believe we deserve abundance. So it's our own damn fault if we're poor.

Okay, I'm exaggerating slightly, but not much. The idea of personal responsibility—in which, by the way, I very much believe—is often carried to an absurd extreme in the self-help biz. I can tell you from experience that being able to visualize clearly the job or salary you want really can help make it happen. But material abundance in mass quantities is not necessarily a measure of our success as spiritual beings. Sometimes we find greater fulfillment with less material abundance in our lives.

Which brings me to the second trendy approach to money and spirituality: the Simplify Your Life movement. According to this approach, too much abundance is bad for our souls because it means we devote too much of our time and energy to getting and spending. If we can just strip away all that material excess, we'll be able to Let Our Inner Light Shine and get in touch with the simple things that really matter. We'll also be doing more good for our planet by cutting down on such things as SUV emissions.

Only in the richest country on Earth, where children have their own computers and teenagers have their own cars and there's a TV in every room of every house telling us we need to buy more and more stuff, could there possibly be such a thing as a Simplify Your Life movement. Now that I think about it, only in the richest country on Earth could we accuse ourselves of not being sufficiently spiritual if we can't create our own abundance. Compared to most of the people on the planet, we're positively choking on abundance.

I'm not trying to make you feel guilty for having food in your belly and a roof over your head. I'm just saying that in this world, the material world, "enough" is a relative term. Money is not in itself good or evil; it is a necessary commodity. As I said, it buys freedom—the freedom to think about your spiritual well being, among other things. We all need to believe we can create our own abundance; we also need to be wary of making abundance our only goal in life.

All we ever really need to earn is enough—enough to cover our living expenses, provide for emergencies, and pay for the things that matter most to us, like our children's educations. If our paychecks don't cover these necessities, insufficiency becomes our whole life; all we can think about is not having enough money, and needing to somehow get enough. If we *can* afford the necessities, we start worrying about whether we have enough for the extras: the hobbies we're passionate about, the causes we deem worthy, the occasional good restaurant meal.

That's the tricky part: Our idea of enough changes as we become older and more prosperous. I don't think of myself as a materialist, but I definitely invest in more expensive clothes and shoes than I used to when I was younger and poorer. That word "invest" is usually a tip-off that I'm spending more than I really need to; but there's a certain practicality, not to mention aesthetic pleasure, in owning good stuff. I'm glad I don't have to buy cardboard furniture anymore. My comfort level has changed.

I'm fully aware, though, that I could give away quite a bit of my stuff and still be perfectly happy. I've taken pay cuts more than once in order to pursue work that seemed closer to my heart's desire. The heart's desire is a work in progress. Sometimes it takes years and years to give yourself permission to know what you really want. Wherever you are in this process, I think it's important to explore your own feelings and beliefs about your idea of "enough."

So I ask again: How much money is enough—for you? When you collect your paycheck every week or two, are you conscious of having earned the freedom to create this segment of your life? How much abundance does it take to make you happy? Could you be just as happy with less? How do you measure your own comfort level?

I have a friend who, after enduring a harrowingly poor childhood, earned a degree in chemistry and obtained a job at a large chemical manufacturing company. Gradually she worked her way up the ranks of management, increasing her income as she went, until she attained solid financial security. But she didn't feel secure. Having stared poverty in the face as a child, she never lost her old fear of it. So she devised a little ritual to reassure herself that she was really, truly earning enough: Every time she got a raise, she'd compute her new hourly wage, then divide that by twelve to figure out how much money she earned every five minutes. She wanted to know how much she was being paid to go to the ladies' room. This, for some reason, was her personal measure of security: The more money they paid her to pee, the more secure she felt.

Whenever I start a new job, I, too, get out the calculator and figure out how the new income compares with the old one. I do this to reassure myself that I'll still be able to feel good about my paycheck, even if I'm earning less than I did before. I need to know I can meet my psychic comfort level as well as my financial one. But my psychic comfort level, unlike my financial comfort level, is not directly proportional to my income. It has more to do with my belief that I can take care of myself, and that, on a deeper level, I am enough in my own soul.

This probably sounds simplistic. But all of us have deep beliefs about our own enoughness, often stemming from childhood, and these beliefs directly affect the way we feel about our paycheck. I have come to believe you can't possibly feel like you're making enough money—no matter what your income level—unless you feel like you're sufficient in your own soul.

You are sufficient, of course. But you don't necessarily feel it one hundred percent of the time. Most of us are deeply conversant with our own insufficiencies; we know exactly where and how we fall short. Feeling our sufficiency—our intrinsic enoughness—is quite another matter. It means connecting with our own wholeness. One of the greatest paradoxes of following a spiritual path is that at the same time we're seeking wholeness, we are already whole on some level. At the same time we seek a connection with the divine, we're already connected.

Exercise: Am I Enough?

Here's a meditation, but it doesn't have to be a formal one. Just make a quiet space for yourself in whatever way you like: Choose a quiet moment, with no distractions, and still your mind as best you can. Then ask yourself this question: Am I enough?

Observe what happens to your breath, your body, your mind, your emotions, at the instant you ask. It's very possible that part of you will panic. This panic is your teacher. If there's an irrational part of you that believes you're not enough, or is afraid you're not enough, ask it to speak, and just listen. Or just feel your way into it.

Find a way to explore the irrational part of you that believes, perhaps, that you don't work hard enough, or you're just not smart, energetic, or worthy enough. If there's a place in your soul where you secretly believe you don't measure up—and many of us have such a place—you need to observe it, let it speak, and challenge it. If it doesn't speak in words, just observe the way it feels. The mere act of observing it will lessen its power.

Say to yourself: *I can face the fear of not being enough, because I really am enough.* If you don't believe it, say it anyway, and say it often. It's true whether you believe it or not.

Find ways to remind yourself—not just in meditation, but through the course of each day—of your own enoughness.

Remember that you are alive and present in your own body, that you have your own feelings, that you love.

Find small, simple ways to feel enoughness in your life. This really is an easy one. I love nothing better, for example, than being able to take a hot shower in the morning. It makes me feel like the richest person on earth. One bite of a really good chocolate mousse is almost more enoughness than I can bear. Or sometimes I'm awakened at night by the sound of one husband snoring and two cats purring. This, too, is more than enough, and (usually) worth the lost sleep.

I suppose I'm talking about feeling grateful, but I'm also talking about simply being present in your body and your life. Once you know the little things that make you feel you have enough, you'll have more of an instinctive sense about whether your working life also makes you feel that way. From the small satisfactions your job provides to the literal payoff of your paycheck, you'll be able to ask yourself, "Is this enough for me?" and be able to give yourself an answer that's grounded in your own truth.

> ### Mantra for the Bad Days:
> Right now, in this moment, I am enough. My own soul is sufficient. And I'm pretty sure there's a KitKat bar in my desk drawer.

Chapter 4

So... What Do You Do?

KEYWORD

vocation

Try this little thought experiment: At a party, you meet someone incredibly articulate and attractive. You feel instinctively that this total stranger is someone you could get along with, someone you'd like to know better. And then you ask, "So... what do you do?" The reply is:

a) "I'm a surgeon."
b) "I'm an accountant."
c) "I'm a conductor." (Meaning orchestras.)
d) "I'm a conductor." (Meaning the 5:49 train to Poughkeepsie.)
e) "I'm in sales, but I'm between jobs right now."

Quick: How do you feel about this articulate, intriguing person now? Say the answer was a) surgeon. I, for one, would feel impressed and intimidated. This person, after all, got into med school, went through a grueling internship and residency (like those driven, attractive surgeons on TV, no doubt), probably makes a ton of money, and does work that changes people's lives for the better—unless this person is a cosmetic surgeon, in which case I imagine that he or she is staring at my neck and thinking I'd look better with a face lift. I have a lot of preconceptions about surgeons. Also about accountants, conductors, and currently unemployed sales people. The habit of pigeonholing people by their means of livelihood is strongly ingrained, and it dies hard. Not incidentally, we also tend to pigeonhole ourselves this way.

"What do you do?" is maybe the second or third question we ask, or are asked, when we meet someone for the first time. The answer determines quite a bit about how we feel about that person, or vice versa. Even if we consider ourselves enlightened enough to care more about who people are than about what they do, it's difficult not to confuse the two. When people ask us what we do, it often feels as though they're really asking, "Who are you?" or, more accurately, "Who do you think you are?"

Are we what we do? Of course not. If you knew that tomorrow were your last day on Earth, I'm willing to bet you wouldn't spend it at the office. Even if you had work you truly loved, you'd probably want to be with the *people* you truly loved.

Human connections have a way of winning out over vocational passions in the end. And yet . . . and yet . . . a true vocation *is* a kind of human connection. It connects us to our truest selves and thus, in a way, to everyone else on the planet. Our idea of vocational bliss is to identify deeply with what we do, to work at something that expresses the best and deepest in us. Few of us get to do this in any sustained, remunerative way. Most of us struggle to bring our deeper selves and our gainfully employed selves closer together, or even into the same ballpark.

How do you feel when someone asks what you do? What are you saying about yourself when you answer? What words do you use to describe yourself, and how do you feel when you speak them?

I've always felt a certain discomfort when I get this question. When I was a music student, at a well-known conservatory where I felt out of place a lot of the time, I'd simply answer, "I'm a singer." I knew that nonmusicians would be impressed by this, especially since I was a classical singer (classical music . . . wow). I knew my fellow music students would not be particularly impressed, singers being a dime a dozen, unless I also told them I was studying with one of the more impressive, career-fostering teachers, which I wasn't. My objective was to find the shortest possible combination of words that would make people think they knew who I was and leave me alone. My answer was a lie; I wasn't really a singer. Yes, I was studying singing with the presumed intention of doing it for a living someday. But I was not a performer in my soul and I knew it. I didn't even like singing "Happy Birthday" in public. "I'm a singer" was a kind of smoke screen behind which I cringed, clueless about who I actually was. I knew I was passionate about music and that I had a talent for it. But how could music be my vocation if I didn't really want to make a living at it?

In recent years, I have worked as a magazine editor, and overall, I've found this a better, truer answer to the "What do you do?" question. It, too, is impressive to many people, especially since they've usually heard of the magazines I've worked for. I like editing. It's a craft that involves making other people's writing look good, a behind-the-scenes profession that suits my temperament much more than performing would have. It pays decently, too. So I can look at my professional life and honestly say I've found a way to support myself that uses my talents creatively and rewardingly. But a magazine editor is not what I *am*, any more than a singer is what I am. I am, among other things, someone who loves words, someone who loves music, and someone who loves, period. None of these is a socially acceptable answer to "What do you do?"

"Socially acceptable," of course, is a key concept here. All our lives we're bombarded with messages about what it means to be a responsible member of society—how much money we're supposed to make, how high we're supposed to want to rise in whatever hierarchy we find ourselves steered into. From earliest childhood, we're asked what we want to be when we grow up, and sometime between adolescence and adulthood, we're expected to be able to produce a serious answer. We need to know, because it affects the courses we take and the schools we apply to. We are encouraged, with good reason, to plan careers that take advantage of the opportunities of the moment. And unless we have an unquenchable desire to paint, or heal the sick, or bake bread, or make music—a true vocation, in other words—we usually try to shoehorn ourselves into these available opportunities. But there is always an underlying tension between the need to function as part of a homogenous social collective and the equally great need to follow our own inner guidance and develop as an individual soul.

Well, guess what: Your soul knows more than society does about who you really are and what you really do. Furthermore, it doesn't matter *what* profession you wind up in. If you heed the call of your own developing soul, if you really listen to what it's trying to tell you throughout your working life, then you're following your true vocation. Maybe you're not being called to become a great artist, physician, or statesman, but believe me, you're being called—called to do the work of becoming who you are. It turns out to be the most important work there is.

My friend Sybil found this out in her early twenties. When I first met her in music school, she seemed to have a real calling as a singer—everybody thought she did, anyway. Her voice wasn't enormous, but it was beautiful. She was intensely musical and could induce a hushed rapture in her audiences. None of us, including Sybil, noticed that she lacked the one thing every aspiring singer needs (besides a good voice): the thick-skinned, steel-spined determination to succeed no matter what.

In fact, Sybil was ambivalent about embarking on a singing career. So many people, including me, had told her what enormous gifts she had that she was almost able to ignore the small, nagging inner voice telling her she was headed down the wrong pike. Yet the facts were all before her. Though she had no problems with stage fright, Sybil really didn't like being looked at. The aspect of an entire audience turning their heads toward her felt like an invasion of her privacy. And she secretly hated singing high notes—not because she couldn't do it, but because high notes seemed to lift her off her feet and right out of her body in a way that made her feel uncomfortably ungrounded. (If it's possible to be a *basso profundo* trapped in the body of a soprano, Sybil was one.) For her, the whole experience of singing felt like walking a high wire without a net, having to maintain perfect control at every moment for no good reason. It felt, in other words, like being someone other than the person she really was.

Sybil hadn't articulated this to herself in so many words. Her parents and friends had always been so proud of her musical achievements that she'd grown up thinking she should feel equally proud of them. Besides, singing was a worthy thing, an artistic thing, the sort of noble occupation she was supposed to want to aspire to. Except she didn't.

When Sybil left the conservatory and tried to make a living in the real world, it became easier for her to admit her true feelings. For one thing, she had a hard time finding work, as all sopranos do. When she did find work, it often seemed like too much effort for too little money, in the service of an art she wasn't sure she loved. The last straw came when she landed a prestigious job teaching singing at a well-known music school (for peanuts, of course) and found herself hating every minute of it. This was when Sybil asked herself the questions that ultimately liberated her: *Why do I hate this so much? Exactly what do I hate about it? Is there anything I'd rather be doing?*

This is the point in the story where you probably expect me

to tell you that Sybil went into business and became wildly successful. Well, no. Sybil moved to New York, became a legal secretary, and set about creating the kind of low-profile life she wanted. She did her job well, and made enough money to pursue the activities that interested her, which did not include singing. Several of her musician friends dropped her when she stopped performing; some expressed anger that she had turned her back on her great gift. But the truth was that Sybil started being happy when she walked away from music. It was the first time she had ever really stood up for who she was and what she wanted. This, to her, was a greater achievement than forging a singing career. She has built her entire adult life on the self-knowledge and self-confidence it gave her.

The point I'm trying to make here is that, as Little Buttercup sings in *H.M.S. Pinafore,* things are seldom what they seem. Your career can be going great guns and bringing you all kinds of money and prestige, but it won't fulfill you if you're running your life in a way that ignores your soul's deeper needs. Conversely, you can work at a seemingly unimpressive job that gives you exactly what you want and need right now both spiritually and professionally. It's not what you do for a living that matters; it's what kind of consciousness you bring to the work you do.

Exercise: So ... what do you *really* do?

How, exactly, do you listen to what your soul is trying to tell you?
Start by paying attention to whatever brings you joy. I'm serious
about this; there's no spiritual barometer like joy.

Think for a moment about your job—your current answer to
the "What do you do?" question. Ask yourself: What aspects of
this job make me happiest? These can be specific tasks, like bal-
ancing the books every month, or running a staff meeting. Or
they can be random things like checking your e-mail in the
morning or organizing your desk in the afternoon. Or they can be
atmospheric things: the adrenaline rush of meeting a deadline or
averting a crisis; the pleasure of working with people you like; the
satisfaction of changing something for the better.

List all the things about your job that make you happy, even if
it's in a small, peripheral way. If you can't think of anything that
induces actual happiness, look for the things that give you a little
shot of energy. Then ask yourself: How is this thing I *do* an expression of the person I *am?* What is it about this task that makes me
feel connected to my deeper self?

Okay, an example: Jane is one of the few magazine editors I know
who actually enjoys cutting copy. When she's presented with a

story that's running long and told she has to cut a bunch of paragraphs or columns to make it fit, she gets a gleam in her eye, sits down at her trusty computer, and starts slashing. Many editors find making cuts a chore, but Jane finds it exhilarating. "When I'm done with this story," she'll say, "Nobody's going to miss what I cut out." And nobody does. Jane's exhilaration comes, in part, from her being at the top of her craft as an editor, from her love of being able to make words do whatever she wants. On a deeper level, Jane is someone who likes to find the real essence of things, to cut away superfluous matter and get to the truth. At heart, she believes that the simplest, shortest way to express something is the most powerful. This is why she loves this part of her work; it expresses the truth-seeker in her.

You see where I'm going with this. The tasks you find enjoyable tell you something crucial about who you really are and what you really care about. If you remind yourself of the things you love about your job, even the little, seemingly dumb things, you'll be bringing what you do and who you are that much closer together.

Mantra for the Bad Days:

I'm the jewel. The job's just the setting.

Chapter 5 The Slough of Suckiness

········ KEYWORD ········
wallowing

If you have never, ever had a day when you thought, even momentarily, "This job sucks!" skip this chapter. You're either incredibly lucky or in total denial, and in either case I don't want to mess with you. Speaking for myself, I've had entire months when I've thought there was something distinctly sucky about my job, even if it was a "good" job. I've been fed up with the task in front of me, cross with my coworkers, pissed off at my boss, frustrated with the corporate culture, or all of the above. And I'm pretty sure I've had good reason to be cross, fed up, pissed off, and frustrated at least some of the time. There is no job that does not, at some moment, in some way, suck. I remind you that as incarnate beings, we're dealing with our own imperfections—and everyone else's—so suckiness is part of the deal.

You can experience the job suckiness of the moment in two ways: asleep or awake. Or, if you prefer, mindlessly or mindfully. You have to deal with the difficulty at hand one way or the other, but the quality of consciousness you bring to it can make an enormous difference in the way it affects you.

Here's a real-life example. I've disguised the identities of the people involved, but you've probably witnessed similar situations. Leslie is Hal's immediate supervisor in a pressure-cooker of an office. The two basically respect and even like each other, but they're not exactly pals, and the stress of trying to meet their deadlines with a small staff and a tight budget has left them both very tense. Leslie's boss, meanwhile, is under pressure from *his* bosses to cut costs and increase efficiency, and he's passing that pressure on to her in the grand corporate tradition of trickle-down anxiety.

One of Hal's ongoing beefs with his job is that he thinks Leslie is a lousy manager, self-indulgent, and overemotional. His judgment is confirmed one morning when Leslie, smarting under a reprimand from her boss, accuses Hal of turning in sloppy work and, in front of the whole department, picks up a report he's written—a report she's already read and approved —and flings it right at him, hitting him in the chest. Then she stalks off. Everybody, including Hal, is shocked into silence.

Leslie has clearly had a meltdown and she's clearly out of line, and Hal clearly has to respond somehow. He can think of two courses of action right off the bat. The first is to report the incident to Human Resources and hope their counsel is not totally useless. The second is to wait a few hours, maybe even a day, and confront Leslie himself, letting her know her behavior was inappropriate and making some sort of attempt to work things out between them. Hal is prepared to do both. But first, he has a little meltdown of his own. "Leslie is a terrible manager," he tells himself. "She feels threatened by me, and she never lets management see how good I am, so I'm never going to get promoted. I shouldn't have to put up with her craziness. I should never have taken this job in the first place. But how can I find another job now, during a recession? But I *have* to. I'm just not challenged here. This place sucks. It's a dead end. Why did I ever get into this business? What am I doing with my life?"

Note that in a few short sentences, Hal has gone from feeling justifiably upset and angry at Leslie's behavior to beating himself up for every career choice he's ever made. He hasn't even noticed that he's moved from experiencing the specific job suckiness of the moment to bewailing the general job suckiness of his entire life. He's fallen headfirst into the Slough of Suckiness, where if one thing sucks, *everything* has to suck. Tell me you haven't been there.

The Slough is a very familiar place for Hal. All his hot-button issues are there: his feelings about authority figures, especially women; his nagging fear that he's made the wrong career choice; his perennial low-level worry that he'll lose his job; his secret belief that all jobs suck and he'll never be happy as long as he has to work. All these are big, thorny issues, and that's the perverse beauty of the Slough. When you face all your demons in one amorphous mass, they're so overwhelming you become absolutely paralyzed. *So you don't have to* do *anything.* You just get to wallow.

When Hal starts telling himself he's in a dead-end job and he's wasting his life, etc., he's avoiding the problem at hand, which is much more mundane: He has a conflict with a single human being, Leslie, who also happens to be his boss. The fact that she's clearly in the wrong doesn't make the situation any less tricky. He'll have to choose his words carefully when he talks to Human Resources, and even more carefully when he talks to Leslie. He's not looking forward to either conversation. Nor is he guaranteed a satisfactory resolution to the problem. Anything might happen. Leslie might pretend to be contrite but secretly be so incensed at Hal for speaking up that she vows to make his life a living hell. Or she might melt down completely and have to leave the company, in which case Hal could wind up with her job—or with a new boss who's even worse. Or Leslie and Hal might have a serious talk that leaves their relationship stronger—or more fragile. The outcome, in other words, is a Great Unknown, compared to which the dank familiarity of the Slough is almost comforting.

The only way to face a Great Unknown is with your eyes wide open. If Hal continues to wallow in his personal Slough of Suckiness, he'll be so distracted by his various demons that he won't be able to pick up signals from the real people right in front of him. He needs to focus on the problem of the moment and save the demons for another time. Sufficient unto the day is the job suckiness thereof.

And how, exactly, is Hal supposed to do this? By learning what the Slough feels like, and making the small but significant choice not to wallow in it. It's a choice he'll have to make again and again, because wallowing is a habit that dies hard.

How do you learn what your Slough of Suckiness feels like? That's easy. To put it bluntly, it feels like the same old shit, the circle you've gone around a thousand times without ever feeling any better. The Slough is never specific; it's always deadeningly vague. And hopeless: There's never a way out. There is, however, some sort of familiar refrain: *This place sucks. My boss is a jerk. This work is meaningless. I'm in the wrong job. I'm in the wrong career. I'm not happy.* Sometimes this refrain is so habitual you don't even hear it, and it requires an effort of consciousness to focus on it. Once you learn to listen for it, though, it's unmistakable.

Another thing about the Slough: There are always plenty of people willing to jump right in there with you. It would be temptingly easy for Hal to seek out one of his colleagues for a mutual bitchfest about Leslie, who really is a trying boss. In practically any workplace, in fact, it's usually pretty easy to find something to bitch about. When times get tough and budgets get tight, management gets scared; there's nothing like a good old-fashioned hiring freeze to make everybody feel overworked and underappreciated. Even in the best of times there's usually more than enough bullshit to go around: insecure bosses, irrational clients, colleagues who don't carry their weight, arcane bureaucratic procedures designed to make everyone's life harder. Business as usual.

I'm not saying you should pretend these obstacles aren't real; a quick check of your blood pressure should convince you they're real enough. The trick is to give each obstacle the kind of attention and the amount of energy it deserves without letting yourself get pulled into the Slough of Suckiness. It's bad enough if you can't order a box of paper clips without filling out three forms and waiting four weeks; it's even worse if you spend half an hour whipping up your anger by ranting to the nearest colleague about the outrageous office supply situation. Or listening while that colleague rants to you.

Negativity starts at the top. A bad boss, or a company that

doesn't value its employees, can create a pervasively negative atmosphere in the workplace. But that negativity will fester longer, and feel infinitely more toxic, if you hook into it.

More than once, I've worked in departments where a bad boss replaced a good boss. (More about bad bosses later; suffice it to say that there are many kinds of bad bosses but you know them when you work for them). In each case, my colleagues and I went from feeling like valued employees who enjoyed our jobs to feeling like slaves in the pit of hell. Did we bitch about it to each other? You bet. In fact, we had to go through a kind of grieving/bitching period when we mourned the Good Old Days and bemoaned the Bad New Days. But there came a point when the grieving and bitching had to stop so we could clear our heads and consider our options. That point was always instructive. It was the point when the negative situation became an impetus for changing our lives rather than a Slough to wallow in.

. . . .

Exercise: Staying Awake in the Slough of Suckiness

Before you can learn to resist the Slough, you have to learn to recognize its siren song. You'll find it a familiar refrain that harps on all your unresolved career and life issues, whether they apply to the situation at hand or not. If you listen hard, you'll also hear a little voice adding "and there's no way out" to every chorus. Your refrain might go something like this:

> I hate this job (and there's no way out).
> My boss is a bitch (and there's no way out).
> I'm in the wrong field (and there's no way out).
> I need the paycheck (and there's no way out).
> I'm not allowed to be creative here (and there's no way out).
> I don't know what I want to be when I grow up (and there's
>   no way out).

You can practically dance to it. Every line of this refrain represents a major unresolved issue for you—an issue of self-worth, or self-sufficiency; a problem with authority; a desperate longing for an out-of-reach fulfillment. All these issues are real. But if you keep listening to the refrain, you'll become trapped in it. Here's where you have to make that little choice I talked about earlier. Whenever you hear the call of the Slough, tell it: "Not now." You know the refrain; God knows you've heard it before. But this is not the moment to go through the whole litany again. So treat it as if it were a nagging child, or, better yet, a telemarketer: Say "Not now." Say it as often as it takes.

"Not now" implies that there's a "later," but of course there isn't. There's only Now. And Now is when you need to concentrate on the issue at hand. This is the creative part.

Take a moment to ask yourself: What's the *real* issue here? In Hal's case, it's his conflict with his boss, Leslie. As deeply as this conflict resonates in Hal's tortured psyche, he needs to contemplate certain specific actions before he can think about the more global stuff—his resentment of authority, his general unhappiness with his workplace, etc. Right now, Hal needs to assess exactly what happened at the moment when Leslie threw the report at him, and what he wants to do about it. That's a big enough conversation to have with himself without dragging in all that other stuff.

Try to find whatever's setting off *your* refrain. Maybe it's filling out all those paper-clip order forms, or being asked to pick up the slack for a colleague who's home with a sick kid *again,* or sitting down to the most boring task on Earth for the thousandth time. What is the real-life difficulty that triggers your personal refrain of hopelessness?

Whatever it is, trust me: There's a way to break the problem down into components that are small enough to be dealt with. Maybe not solved completely, but addressed in some way. Whatever the situation, there's some part of it you have control over, even if it's only a tiny part. There is some part of this situation that *does* have a way out—a real, doable, attainable way out. Try to find that part.

Suppose, for example, that you're sitting down to that boring task. Before you start telling yourself you're wasting your entire precious life in this dead-end job, think about *what* you hate about the task. Maybe there's a way to do it more efficiently. Or a way to delegate it to somebody else. Or a way to reward yourself for completing it. Maybe there's no way to make the task more bearable—in which case you might legitimately ask yourself, "What would I rather be doing instead? Is there some way to structure my life so I'm doing more of the stuff I'd rather do?" This is a large question, but at least it's a constructive one. The mere act of asking a constructive question is a victory in itself.

You have to learn to pull yourself out of the Slough of Suckiness if you want to ask the constructive questions that can change your life. The difficulty of the moment can be your teacher, but only if you're awake enough to see it for what it is.

Mantra for the Bad Days:

I am exactly where I need to be at this moment. So all I have to do is figure out where the hell I am at this moment.

Chapter 6 Who's the Boss?

······ KEYWORD ······
authority

Once, at one of my magazine jobs, I was asked to sit in for my vacationing boss for a couple of weeks. The minute I stepped into her shoes, I went from being a senior editor to being someone who *edited* senior editors, and my colleagues immediately began treating me very differently. To put it succinctly, they stopped treating me like an equal and started treating me like a parent.

Suddenly, without wanting to, I became the embodiment of all their unresolved authority issues. I noticed, for example, that some editors submitted incomplete work, leaving it to me to make editorial decisions they were perfectly capable of making themselves. One editor who I thought liked and respected me tried to do an end-run around me by submitting copy directly to the editor-in-chief (who of course passed it right back to me). Another, whom I knew to be very experienced, was so insecure and eager to please she made *me* nervous. Still another, who had a tendency to miss her deadlines, started hiding out in her office and ducking my e-mails and phone calls. I couldn't wait to relinquish my temporary authority and become one of the gang again.

What was intriguing, and infuriating, was that my colleagues' reactions to me had nothing to do with our respective abilities and everything to do with the pecking order of the moment. We had worked together as peers for months, but I became a kind of parent figure as soon as I acquired the power to grant or withhold approval of their work—which I suppose isn't all that different, in a way, from a parent's power to reward or punish.

This experience started me thinking about my own response to authority. I had to admit there were times I wanted to make my boss, who was a close friend, into some kind of mommy—either the good kind, who could somehow make all my problems go away, or the bad kind, who was arbitrary and inflexible and simply had to be obeyed. Then I remembered how, when I first entered the working world in my twenties, I simply took it for granted that my bosses had the same make-or-break authority over me that my parents and teachers had once wielded. It took me a long, long time to learn to differentiate between the actual power they had over me as bosses and the power I projected onto them as parent surrogates.

Then I started thinking about authority itself, about how we progress in life from being utterly controlled by an outside authority to finding, trusting, and being guided by our own inner authority. We move (to give a really simplistic example) from being dressed by our parents to choosing and putting on our own clothes. We are educated, if we're lucky, to think for ourselves; and if we do enough thinking, we eventually acquire some degree of confidence in our own ideas. We gain experience at our jobs until we're fairly convinced we know what we're doing. In other words, we grow up.

Except the reality is that we grow up piecemeal. Think about it: I'm sure there are some areas of your life where you feel absolutely confident, whether it's your ability to drive a car or boil an egg, your prowess at closing a deal, or your knack for finding your way around an unfamiliar city or software program. I'm also pretty sure there are things you're not so confident about. I, for instance, think of myself as a total non-athlete, okay, a hopeless klutz. I am not, in fact, a natural athlete, but I'm not really all that klutzy either. I just have very little physical confidence, and this insecurity dates all the way back to my childhood in those long-ago days before Title IX.

Most insecurities, obviously, have their roots in childhood. Stuff happens to us as kids or adolescents, and we spend the rest of our lives getting over it. My point is that our insecurities—those areas where we don't trust our own authority—represent deep personal issues, issues we're still working on. Of course, we bring those authority issues with us to the workplace. And there's nothing like having a boss to bring them to the surface, whether we're conscious that this is happening or not.

Being conscious of our authority issues is preferable to not being conscious of them, but it doesn't make those issues disappear. That, I'm afraid, takes patience, practice, and the willingness to face oneself honestly, like everything else. My friend Alex, for example, is all too conscious of her biggest authority issue. "When people come at me with an attitude of 'prove yourself,' I lose my ability to stay calm," she says. "It's got something to do with my father; I get ineffective, tongue-tied, and frazzled. If someone approaches me with an attitude of peer-hood and respect, I perform well. But I can't predict when that's going to happen, so I go into new situations feeling very anxious."

What, exactly, is Alex supposed to do about this? Well, for starters, she can give herself credit for having gotten this far in understanding herself. Had she not achieved this level of awareness, she would simply feel frazzled and tongue-tied around her bosses without knowing why. So chalk one up for old Alex. The problem is that she feels stuck at this point. She's already worked with a therapist to uncover some of her feelings about her father, and she's pretty sure she understands those feelings, at least in part. So why can't she just get past them? Why does she still freeze up at the prospect of being asked to prove herself?

One reason, clearly, is that Alex has felt anxious in the presence of authority for so long that she's become anxious about feeling anxious. She's so used to being scared she'll be asked to prove herself, in other words, that she now gets scared in advance. It's a reflex, a habit. She probably did it through her entire childhood, and she's still doing it now. Habits, as we all know, are neither made nor broken overnight. So the first thing Alex can do is to observe that she has this habit and cut herself a little slack—or, you might say, show herself a little compassion. And the second thing she can do is start questioning, gently, whether she still needs this particular habit—whether she has not, perhaps, outgrown it. The next time she feels herself getting anxious, she might tell herself something like, "Hey, I'm *good* at what I do. I have a lot of experience at this kind of work. If I don't do it perfectly the first time, I know I'll get it right the second or third time. And I know it isn't the end of the world if I'm not perfect. So do I really need to freak out like this?"

Note that this little conversation has nothing to do with Alex's boss, or her clients, or any outside person asking her to prove herself. It's all about Alex learning to connect with her inner authority. Suppose, for example, that Alex's boss (or client) really is aggressive and belligerent, and really does ask Alex to prove herself. It makes no difference: Alex still needs to prove herself to *Alex* first. And this will happen gradually, because growing up happens gradually, and the part of Alex that gets anxious about authority is a part of her that's still growing up. Every time her old feelings of anxiety come to the surface, she can take it as an opportunity to remind herself that she isn't a child anymore and she knows what she's doing. Sooner or later, she'll even believe it.

One other thing. The way we respond to authority, past or present, is directly related to the way we engage in our own spiritual practice, whatever form that practice may take. Our authority issues affect the way we pray, the way we perceive ourselves, the way we follow our own path.

Think for a moment about how you felt about God—the

ultimate authority—when you were a child. Be as honest with
yourself as you can. There is no "right" answer to this. What
were you told about God by your parents, friends, or religious
teachers, and what was your inner response? Belief? Skepti-
cism? Obedience? Rebellion?

I, for example, attended Sunday school in a Reform Jewish
synagogue, where I learned that God was a loving and occasionally wrathful Father who picked on everyone except the
Jews, except when He picked on the Jews. I also learned that
God was everywhere and that you couldn't define Him, so He
certainly didn't have a human son named Jesus, not that there
was anything wrong with Jesus, who, by the way, was Jewish.

Granted, this was a fairly confusing message, but the one big
thing that came through clearly was that God had life and
death power over me, so I'd better watch my ass. This God was
masculine, paternal, and remote—the biggest Big Daddy there
was—and I might or might not measure up to His scrutiny.
One of the prayers in the liturgy went, "May the words of my
mouth and the meditations of my heart be acceptable in Thy
sight, O Lord," which signified to me that there was a good
chance my words and meditations might *not* be acceptable.
This God was not necessarily on my side. Well, I wasn't always
sure my parents and teachers were on my side, either.

While I was growing up, I also had genuine spiritual experiences, as I believe every child does, of awe, mystery, and terrifying joy. None of these experiences took place anywhere near my synagogue, though I kept hoping to find them there. Instead I encountered them in nature, music, poetry, and, later on, in love. Since I wanted to seek God—this was always a given for me, for some reason—I eventually decided to be guided by these living experiences of awe and joy, and by my own good, skeptical mind. It seemed to me that the things I was taught about spirituality by outside authorities had to be ratified, somehow, by my own direct experiences of Spirit. Otherwise, they were someone else's teachings and nothing more.

My path could have been very different. I could, for example, have had genuine spiritual experiences within my family's faith rather than outside it. I could have rejected spirituality altogether in childhood and come back to it later in life. Or not. I could have sought God in any one of an infinite number of ways, there being as many paths to God as there are people. My point is that growing up spiritually, like growing up emotionally or professionally, involves learning to find our own way, not just doing as we're told. A spiritual path is, among other things, a confrontation with authority. It involves our confronting whatever religious authority we grew up with and deciding which teachings and experiences ring true for us. It is our own inner authority that helps us listen for this ring of truth, and that guides us to follow the truth in our own way. Even if we decide to follow one specific faith or set of teachings to the letter, we need to make this decision as grownups—of our own free will. If we're doing it for an outside authority, we're not doing it for ourselves. ("If I am not for myself, who will be for me?" said the Jewish sage Hillel. "And if not now, when?")

Dealing with our personal authority issues in the workplace may not seem to have much to do with forging a spiritual path. But think about it: Your confrontations with bosses and subordinates bring you face to face with your feelings about your power over others and theirs over you; about having, or not having, the freedom to make your own decisions; about being asked to prove yourself. Tell me these aren't spiritual issues! Anything that helps you connect with your inner authority— including the seemingly mundane realization that we sometimes make our bosses into substitute parents—helps you grow as a spiritual being.

Okay, an example. I've changed the names here, but I've actually witnessed this situation: Audrey sells advertising space in a magazine. Sales representatives are independent sorts, and Audrey deeply resents the guidelines her boss, Janis, has established for making presentations to clients, negotiating rates, and closing deals. Janis's guidelines are, in fact, fairly sensible and reasonable, but Audrey can't stand being told what to do. So she simply makes deals as she sees fit, occasionally getting into hot water by making promises she can't exactly keep. When Janis reprimands her for her reckless sales tactics, Audrey gets defensive, saying, "I'm the most productive person in this department. You couldn't make your quotas without me." This happens to be true, but it doesn't make Audrey's behavior any less exasperating.

Glen, another sales rep in the same department, follows Janis's guidelines to the letter. In fact, he makes a fetish of obeying every rule, asking Janis for permission every time he wants to do something the tiniest bit offbeat. Janis always tells him to follow his own instincts, but he can't seem to do it without consulting her first.

Both Audrey and Glen are excellent salespeople, and both of them want to make poor Janis their parent—Audrey by being a Bad Girl and Glen by being a Good Boy. If Audrey could stop seeing herself as a rebel for five minutes, she might actually learn something from Janis and, not incidentally, relax a little.

As it is, she can only experience her own power when she's challenging Janis's. If Glen could stop asking for Janis's permission all the time, he might allow himself to grow into his own independence. If he could stop trying so hard to be good, in other words, he might learn how good he actually is.

Exercise: Who Do I Think I'm Reporting To?

Think about your boss, or, more accurately, about your response to your boss. For the purposes of this exercise, it doesn't really matter whether said boss is the most enlightened person you've ever worked for or the biggest jackass on the planet. What matters is how you react to him or her.

Think about a part of your job you do particularly well, some task you feel confident about and take pleasure in. Picture yourself doing this task and enjoying your own mastery of it.

Now picture yourself doing this task with your boss standing behind you and looking over your shoulder. How does your experience of the task change if you believe you're being watched and graded on every tiny piece of it? Do you lose some of your self-confidence? Do you start second-guessing yourself based on what your boss might or might not like about your work? Do you, in other words, start doubting your own authority?

Granted, your boss is probably not right there in the room with you while you're working—at least I hope not—but you've probably internalized him or her to some degree. You know what flies in your workplace and what doesn't, and you can imagine whether or not your boss will approve of what you're doing. This is a good thing. What I'd like you to think about is whether you feel you and your boss are both adults working for a common good, or whether you sometimes react as though you're a child and your boss is your parent.

Ask yourself:

- In what ways, or under what circumstances, do I treat my boss as a parent—someone to be either placated or rebelled against?
- Do I give this person a power over me that he or she doesn't really possess?
- Do I ever forget that we're both grownups with grownup abilities and grownup lives?
- Am I, perhaps, relating to my boss in ways I've actually outgrown?
- How far do I trust my inner authority to do my own job—or to know when I need to ask for help?

While you're thinking about all this, pose yourself one more question: How far do I trust my inner authority to follow my own spiritual path? Don't worry about coming up with a definitive answer to this one right away. But do, by all means, ask.

> **Mantra for the Bad Days:**
> My boss is not my parent. I am not a child.
> And I have the paycheck to prove it.

Chapter 7

Working and Praying

Don't worry. I'm not going to presume to tell you how—or where, or when, or what—to pray. Nor am I going to assume that you and I necessarily mean the same thing by the word "prayer." Prayer is deeply personal, maybe the most personal thing there is. What I want to explore here is whether it's possible, or even desirable, to engage in your chosen form of prayer at work.

I think it's both possible and desirable. In fact, I think it's almost inevitable, because to me, prayer is any kind of dialogue between the human and the divine, and I believe we carry at least some spark of the divine within us. When we make any attempt to be present for our own lives, to experience our whole selves, we are embracing both our humanity and our divinity. Our mere existence is a kind of prayer. Not that it always feels that way.

You may not agree with me about this. Indeed, the first dictionary definition of "pray" is "to entreat or implore . . . to request in a humble manner." This sounds, on first reading, like flat-out begging. That was my childhood understanding of prayer: as a plea to an external, paternal God who could bless me, give me the stuff I wanted, and possibly vanquish my tribe's enemies (whoever they were—maybe the Communists) in exchange for my being a good girl. I'm not really talking about this type of transaction, where the pray-er begs for some kind of reward from the pray-ee. But I do believe prayer is, first and foremost, an entreaty—a humble request that the divine be present for us right here, right now, and that *we* be present for the divine. The second dictionary definition of "pray" comes closer to this idea: "to address God or a god with adoration, confession, supplication, or thanksgiving." To talk to God— whatever we mean by God—in whatever way we choose, with or without making any specific requests. To have a conversation, a dialogue, with the divine, wherever we find it.

Talking to God—calling the divine into the present moment—is not something you need to save for formal meditation or prayer. I think it has a place in every area of one's life, even work. Especially work. When you take a moment to open an inner door to the idea of the divine, you acknowledge the possibility that your life has a larger design than the physical reality before you—your office walls, your "to do" list, your telephone. You remind yourself that you are more than what you do. You enable yourself to perceive the nobility in seemingly mundane endeavors. And you summon strengths and insights you didn't know you possessed. Prayer is an enormously creative act.

How, exactly, are you supposed to open this inner door to the possibility of the divine during the course of an average workday? Actually, there's more than one door. There are probably as many doors as there are conscious beings, and your form of prayer, whatever it is, is your personal door.

If you're comfortable with the idea of invoking divinity—of talking to God—you probably already have your own vocabulary of prayer. It might, then, feel perfectly natural to you to take a few moments during the workday to utter actual prayers to yourself, silently or aloud: "I pray to bring my best self to this work," or "I pray to understand what this difficult situation is trying to teach me," or "I align myself with the divine presence within me."

You already know the words that resonate for you. I'm only going to suggest you remember to say them in what might seem like odd times and places: when you're sitting down to work you find daunting or thankless; when you're attending a mind-numbing staff meeting; when you're facing a difficult interaction with a colleague or client. I have a friend who simply says "Blessed be," silently or aloud, when she wants to remember that we all have the capacity to bring a blessing into being. I sometimes pray just to be fully present, divinity, humanity, and all: "I don't really want to be here. But please, help me *be* here." Or, more simply: "Here I am."

Words are powerful things. The mere act of saying or thinking the words of a prayer can put you into a prayerful state. If you're not comfortable with the idea of formal prayer, you can simply ask to be open to the idea of a greater reality, and leave it at that. Your readiness to consider the possibility of the divine is itself an act of prayer. But please don't force it. If words like "God" and "divine" make you squirm, nobody's saying you have to use them. This is your spiritual path, not someone else's, and you get to choose the practices that connect you with your own spirituality—*whatever that means for you*.

Besides, as I'm sure you know, there are many wordless practices—breathing exercises, meditation techniques—that can help center you and nourish your spiritual being. I'm not suggesting that you meditate for long stretches at work. Deep meditative states are not wildly compatible with the average workplace (and heaven help you if the phone rings). But you might want to devote a few minutes to centering yourself at various times during the day, with the express purpose of reminding yourself that there's more to you than your work-load. What if you're so busy you can't possibly take time to center yourself? Do it anyway. The times you feel the most frantic are the times you most need to coax yourself back into your body and soul, even if it's only for half a minute.

Shut your door, if you have one, or just close your eyes, and do whatever it takes to bring yourself to a place of inner still-ness. Maybe you have a favorite breathing exercise that reli-ably calms you down. There are dozens of these. One centering yoga technique, for example, is to inhale through your nose for a count of seven; hold your breath for a moment; exhale through your nose for a count of seven; hold your breath for a moment; and repeat the cycle several times. It really doesn't matter how you arrive at stillness; the stillness itself is the point. When you attend to what Oscar Wilde once called the Great Silence, you connect with a source of enormous strength and support. Don't take my word for this; run the experiment for yourself.

Perhaps you have another way of finding your center. My

friend Joan, who has two kids and a demanding career as a pathologist, centers herself by sneaking out for walks in the woods. Even if she can only manage it once a month, she knows she needs to wrap herself in the silence of nature, which to her is a holy silence.

Look, I'm well aware that the average life is not set up for silence. This is especially true if you're a parent. If there's any empty space in a parent's day, a dozen things rush in to fill it. You're frantic at work, and then you come home to your kids and feel you somehow need to make up the hours you've missed with them. You want to help them with their homework, get involved in their activities, and spend "quality" time with them. That's fine. But have you ever thought about spending empty, dopey, utterly *pointless* time with your kids? The kind where you just hang out together without having to accomplish anything? There's growing evidence that unscheduled family time is just as important for kids, maybe more important, than rigidly scheduled activities.

When Joan's children were little, she loved to spend evenings lounging on the couch and cuddling them, or watching them play, or letting them jump in and out of her lap. If she was too tired to match their energy, she could at least give them her full presence. Doing so made her feel relaxed, loving, and connected to a sense of greater purpose; it was, in other words, a form of prayer.

There are so many things clamoring for our attention. Do I really have to list them for you? It's not just the pile of stuff on our desks. It's also the stuff at home—all those endless tasks we're responsible for—and, God help us, the stuff in the news media, tidings more urgent and unbearable than those any other generation has ever had to deal with. Do not underestimate the cumulative force of the noise of the world. We are relentlessly bombarded with information, some of it useful, much of it useless, all of it yammering ceaselessly at us via radio, television, print, and our own yammering minds. The noise is so loud we don't even hear it. It distracts us from making contact with our greater selves. It's up to us to make the decision to shut out that noise, if only for a few moments at a time, to ask that the divine be present for us, and that we be present for it.

....

Exercise: Work as Prayer

Work itself can become a form of prayer if you learn to approach it that way. Okay, not *all* work *all* the time—but some work, some of the time.

I used to love practicing the piano. I was never a very good pianist, but I loved the process of learning a new piece. The music lay encoded in those fat black notes on the page; my job was to recreate it in the present moment. To do this, I had to engage in a kind of dialogue with the composer, to try to figure out what he wanted. I also had to coax the notes into my fingers, which did not always respond as I wanted them to. The whole endeavor was a tussle—with the composer, with my own fingers, thoughts, and emotions, and with the music itself. When I actually managed to play a piece well, the music felt like grace, a gift, something I'd managed to retrieve from another place.

You see where I'm headed with this. I'm talking about practice, as in spiritual practice. When you practice prayer or meditation, as when you practice an instrument, you do something both creative and collaborative. You forge your own spiritual path, and you engage in a dialogue with the divine; you invite a greater reality into your consciousness. In stating your readiness to be open to Spirit, you prepare yourself to receive whatever comes. You don't move Spirit—Spirit moves you.

So here's my question: What would happen if you approached an everyday task as though it were a spiritual practice, like praying or making music? What if, when you sat down to write a memo, work on a spreadsheet, or grade a spelling test, you approached it as though this task, too, could be a doorway to your own divinity?

I'm talking about something fairly simpleminded here. A memo is a memo, not a Bach partita, and I'm not asking you to pretend it's more exalted than it is. But even the most mundane chore can be hallowed if you bring your full presence to it. Before you write that memo, pause for a moment to bring your awareness to the task. Try to think of some positive implication of the work you're about to do: "I want to communicate clearly." Or "I want to send a helpful, supportive message." Or "I'm about to impart knowledge that will help others do their jobs." Don't go overboard on this; keep it simple. If you can find absolutely no redeeming feature in the task before you, you might say something like, "Here I am, writing this memo. I want to remember my own worth, and the dignity of my own path." The more inane the task, the more you need to remind yourself that you really are a worthy being.

....

A friend of mine, while preparing dinner one evening—not her favorite activity—suddenly looked at the fish she was about to broil and realized it had given its life so that she could feed her family. She felt no particular guilt for being at the top of the food chain. Being a practical woman, she understood that life needs to feed on life to survive. But standing there in her kitchen in that

quiet moment, she felt something unexpected come over her:
gratitude. She felt grateful for the fish, grateful for her familiar little kitchen, grateful that her family had enough to eat. So before
she seasoned the fish, she thanked it for nourishing her. In that
moment, she felt as though she had both given and received a
blessing.

Well, of course that's the way blessings are. You receive them
by giving them, and vice versa. But first, you need to be present.

Mantra for the Bad Days:

Somewhere within all this noise is an enormous silence. If I just
shut up for a moment, I'll be able to hear it.

Chapter 8

The Dream That Got Away

Five of the saddest words of tongue or pen (to me, anyway): "I'm an Art History major."

The minute I hear them, usually emanating from the lips of a talented and intelligent young woman, I think, "Poor thing. She loves Art, she loves Beauty, and she's going to wind up in some totally unrelated office job wondering how the hell she got there because she's never going to find anything in her field."

Then I think: "No, maybe she'll do better than I did. Maybe she'll get a job as a curator at the Met and live happily ever after on Fifth Avenue."

This, of course, is my own vestigial bitterness talking, the bearable but unbanishable bitterness of the former arts major who doesn't make a living in the arts. There's a lot of it going around, because, as we all know, there are precious few job opportunities in the arts. Any arts major knows that when he or she graduates, the pursuit of beauty ends and the pursuit of a paycheck begins—the dream ends and reality begins.

Of course, arts graduates aren't the only ones who get clobbered by reality. How many former philosophy majors do you know who work as philosophers? Or math majors who earn their keep doing math? The things we do for love are rarely the things we do for money. What I want to know is, what happens to the love? How much of it, if any, do we bring to the jobs that gainfully employ us? Is it even possible to reconcile our youthful dreams with our grownup working life?

I'm aware that these are loaded questions. My friend James, who never wanted anything else except to be a musician, worked for years as a freelance trumpet player. The life was challenging, involving a lot of travel and requiring great physical stamina. (A trumpeter needs the lungs of an athlete, the lips of a great lover, and teeth of steel, among other things.) James loved his work, but after a few years the market tightened and jobs became scarce. Having a wife and child to support, he hung up his horn and found another job, in the commercial end of the music business. He considered himself lucky to be working in music, but he no longer went anywhere near his trumpet. In fact, it was years before he could even sit down and listen to music for pleasure. He couldn't bear to; it brought him too close to the deep feelings that had prompted him to become a musician in the first place. Though he didn't regret giving up the freelance life, he couldn't help thinking of himself as a failed artist. You can move on to other pursuits, but a lost love is a lost love.

Even when you pursue a career dream as far as you can, even if you're satisfied you've done the best you could, it hurts to have to abandon it. Many of us, I venture to say, never pursue our dreams even that far, and that failure of pursuit can hurt even more. We spend our lives wondering whether we could have made a go of it.

My cousin Martin, for example, has some painful unfinished business regarding a very old dream. When he was a boy, he wanted to be an actor or comedian—something flashy, creative, and fun. He certainly had the temperament for it. He was always the class clown, the kind of kid who made his parents laugh even while they were trying to discipline him.

When Martin was 10, he made the mistake of telling his father he wanted to go into show business. His father told him flat out that he didn't have the talent for it and shouldn't even try because he wouldn't succeed. "You're a plodder," he remembers his father telling him. "You're always going to have to work extra hard to make your way in life." I suppose some kids might have taken this as a challenge and set out to prove their father wrong, but Martin, who worshipped his dad, was crushed. If he was doomed to be a plodder, well, he would plod. In college, he starred in theatricals, ran a little radio station, and even wrote some plays of his own. But he never made a serious try at a show business career.

Instead, he got a master's degree in communications and took a series of "safe" corporate jobs which have brought him a measure of success and security, but which basically bore him to death. He misses being able to express the gonzo, class-clown creativity that's such a vital part of him. He'd love to write a television or movie script, but at this point, he has a mortgage and a couple of kids to put through college. So he works, and saves, and plans, and keeps plodding, determined to give his kids the freedom to pursue *their* dreams, whatever they might be. He's not an unhappy man, but his old dream haunts him. Now in his 40s, he still wonders: *What if I'd ignored my father and given it a shot? What if I'd gone out to Hollywood in my 20s and tried to find myself a place in show business?* Martin is not convinced he would have succeeded, but he can't forgive himself for never having tried. To him, the path of his dreams and the path of reality have never come anywhere near each other, let alone crossed.

Except for the unusual cruelty exhibited by Martin's father (and perhaps it's not all that unusual), Martin's story could be almost anyone's: Child, brimming with energy and creativity, declares that he wants to be a (fill in the blank) when he grows up. Parent, understanding that the world is a difficult place where very few people actually become successful (fill in the blank)s, gently steers Child toward some more "realistic" dream. Child, having had the living joy knocked out of him, eventually gets over the "unrealistic" dream, becomes a productive member of society, and lives, if not happily, realistically ever after. Child's energy and creativity either get expressed in some other way, or they don't.

And yes, in case you're wondering, this happened to me, too. When I was about nine, I wrote a letter to the editor of a magazine—okay, a comic book; okay, a *Superman* comic book (ours was an intellectual household)—and showed it to my mother. I was proud of its smart-alecky humor, but she must have thought it was *too* smart-alecky because she tore it up right in front of me, muttering something about how she was afraid we would get sued if I sent it. I've never forgotten how shocked I felt. I don't remember what I said to her, but I do know that I never again tried to write anything for publication, and I sure as hell never showed any more "creative" writing to my mother. In other words, I learned to shut up. It never even occurred to me to dream of working as a writer.

I suppose you could say that any career dream is unrealistic until you make it happen. Every movie star grew up wanting to be a movie star, and we all know how unrealistic that is. Every opera diva wanted to be an opera diva; every great chef wanted to be a great chef; every astronaut wanted to be an astronaut. Somehow, they had the talent, the drive, and the luck (don't forget luck) to succeed, with or without their parents' support, and we admire them for it. We admire them for dreaming dreams that were so overpowering and irresistible they couldn't bear to pursue anything else. Dreams they were willing to suffer for.

Most of the rest of us, in the absence of such a tyrannical and compelling dream or talent, find some way to compromise. Would-be novelists get jobs where writing skills are valued—in public relations, corporate speechwriting, advertising—and wind up feeling both proud of their proficiency in their craft and frustrated that they have to write in someone else's voice. Would-be performers spend their evenings and weekends working in amateur theatricals, and love it. But, I ask again, how much of that love do they bring to their day jobs?

How much love are you *supposed* to bring to your day job?

Does gainful employment have anything to do with love? The very term "day job" has come to connote work that's done for money rather than love, as though the part of you that loves can come out only at night. Well, great. That's eight, nine, or ten hours—daylight hours—when you're putting your love, your joy, your enthusiasm, on hold.

Martin and his workaholic father before him were brought up to believe that fiscal responsibility takes precedence over personal happiness, as though the two were mutually exclusive: Work is hell, but you have to do it, and the harder you work, the more brownie points you can give yourself, with bonus points for ruining your health in the process. If you look around you, you'll see plenty of people busily accruing brownie points. They take pride in their work, but they've had most of the joy knocked out of them in the collision between childhood dreams and grownup reality.

Here is where I am *not* going to tell you that the solution to day-job misery is to find a way to do what you love for a living. There are a number of self-help books purporting to tell you how to do this, and I'm all for it, though I believe it's quite difficult to rearrange your working life in order to do something you love, trusting that money will follow. You may get pretty hungry waiting for money to follow. And in any case, figuring out how to do work you love is a major, long-term project. How do you bring love to the day in front of you, the only day you really have?

....
Exercise: Dreaming on the Treadmill

In a quiet, distraction-free moment, call into your mind a career you used to dream about as a child, teenager, or young adult. Don't censor yourself, even if it's something wildly impractical, like, say, wanting to be a cowboy. I want you to remember how it felt to be in love with the idea of doing something. Spend a little time feeling those feelings once more: wanting to dance, to sing, to act, to write, to dig for dinosaur bones, ride horses, lead safaris, play Major League baseball, or ski in the Olympics. Or wanting to read all day or listen to music all night.

Expect to encounter resistance to feeling these feelings again, especially if this was a dream you pursued with any seriousness. As I said, it hurts to abandon a dream, and remembering it may be painful. You may judge yourself for having failed, or for having dared to dream it at all. Here's where you need to say to yourself: "Failure is not the issue. This is something I loved, and loving is the most essential thing I do. In dreaming this dream, I dared to love, and that, itself, is a kind of success."

Make regular appointments to reconnect with your dream, and each time you do, resist the temptation to judge yourself. Instead, stay focused on how it feels to love the idea of doing something. Tell yourself: "I have a right to this love." Be the person who loves. This is not a small thing; it's a very big thing. I happen to think it's the only thing.

Once you've reconnected with your old dream, I want you to try something truly subversive. Ask yourself: "What would happen if I brought my whole self—including the dreamer—to work?" I am not, repeat, not suggesting you sit at your desk wishing you were a cowboy. I'm suggesting you make a conscious effort to express your own unique and inimitable passion at your office.

Say, for example, you once wanted to be an actor. Next time you're trying to make a point in a staff meeting, you might ask yourself, "What would the actor do right now?" The actor in you might stand up a bit straighter, speak a bit more clearly and compellingly, and make more of an effort to reach out and grab your audience. After all, the fact that you once dreamed of being an actor indicates that something in you wanted to communicate something important, to command attention, to hold the spotlight. You can do all these things without an Actors Equity card.

Say you once dreamed of being a doctor. There's still a would-be healer in you. There are probably dozens of opportunities in any given workday when you can ask yourself, "What would the healer do right now?"

What would the singer in you do? Or the poet? Or the archaeologist? Or the politician? You'll never know until you ask. Martin, for example, has recently taken to letting more of his innate comic genius come out in his corporate presentations. He has a gift for taking people by surprise, and he's discovering that this can liven up a dull presentation like nobody's business. He may not have the show-business career he always dreamed of, but he's beginning to have a fan club at the office.

Remember: If you've ever shut the door on a dream, you've shut the door on an essential part of yourself—on vital energy, on joy. Telling yourself you've failed is a smokescreen, a ploy to keep yourself from going near those painful feelings again. But the original love wasn't painful, it was pleasurable, and you need it in your life. Tell yourself: "This joy is still in me. I need it. I want it in my life right now."

Of course, doing this exercise will make you more acutely aware of how you feel about your current job. Examine these feelings, too, without judging yourself. Resist the temptation to beat up on yourself for not adoring every minute of work (of course you don't). Instead, ask yourself: "How often do I connect with my own capacity for love during the workday? Do I believe that love even *belongs* at the office?"

THE DREAM THAT GOT AWAY

It does belong there, of course. There have been days when I've really, really hated my job but felt redeemed by a sudden, unexpected rush of love for a colleague. I can tell you from experience that when times get tough at work, your feelings of love, however they manifest, are the best, truest things you have.

Mantra for the Bad Days:
I need the stuff my dreams are made of. And so do the bozos who run this place, whether they know it or not.

Chapter 9 Happiness is the Right Rock Pile

········· KEYWORDS ·········

happiness ■ relationship

My friend Jennie is looking for a job. Again. She already has a perfectly good job, mind you. She's just doing what she always does when she starts to feel trapped, unappreciated, or dead-ended: She's updating her resume and beating the bushes.

I know I'm making Jennie sound like some kind of malcontent, but she really isn't. She's very clear-eyed and practical, and she can see that the corporate culture at her current job is structured in such a way that she will never be happy there. She wishes she'd seen this when she accepted the job, but at the time it was an opportunity she couldn't resist at a salary she couldn't refuse. Jennie needs to earn a good salary; she has a lot of financial responsibilities. But she also needs to be happy—it's as high a priority for her as the paycheck. And in her pursuit of happiness, she's changed jobs fairly often.

When Jennie starts a new job, she usually goes through a honeymoon period where she's learning, growing, and loving the challenge before her. Once she masters the job, she cruises for a while, enjoying the ride. After a while, she starts getting bored and restless and wondering where her next challenge will lie. Or the job itself changes: There's a new boss, or a new management policy, that turns her formerly congenial position into something grim and pleasureless. So out comes the resume. Job hunting makes Jennie feel like she's doing something active and positive instead of just sitting there being unhappy. She works in an industry where people move around a lot, so her wanderlust hasn't hurt her career. But by now, she's done the job-search dance a few too many times and been through a few too many honeymoons. Is this, she wonders, all there is? Will I ever settle down in a job for good? Will I ever find a job that's my soul mate?

What a good question. It's never been easy to find the job equivalent of a long, happy marriage, and these days, when job security is no longer a given, we pretty much assume we can't plan on staying in one place forever. So we change jobs, or dream about changing jobs, to attain greater responsibility, higher salaries, sexier titles—and, like Jennie, to seek happiness. It becomes useful, then, to ask ourselves what we're looking for, what happiness actually means to us in this context.

What do we want from a soul mate, anyhow? A soul mate in the Platonic sense . . . Oh, hell, never mind Plato. Open any romance novel, if you can bear it. A soul mate is someone who sees and understands us without our having to explain ourselves, a mirror of all that's best in us. Meeting our soul mate, we imagine, will feel like meeting our other half, the person who completes us—like coming home. We talk of "finding" our soul mate as though it's someone we've already known and lost in the distant past, before we came into this life. This may actually be the case for all I know. All I can say for sure is that we long for a sense of completeness, an answering voice; and we long for it in work as deeply as we long for it in love.

And as in love, we tend to look for this completeness in all the wrong places. By which I mean we carry a certain amount of personal baggage with us in our search for our ideal jobs.

Jennie, for instance, can see in hindsight why she was drawn into the work environment that's now making her so unhappy. "I didn't have a good feeling about the job to begin with," she tells me. "But when I first interviewed with my boss, there was something about her that reminded me of my alcoholic mother and felt deeply familiar and comfortable. I thought this was someone I could work for. After she hired me, of course, she broke every promise she'd made in the interview. She wouldn't let me do what she'd supposedly hired me to do. She didn't really want me to be the person she'd said she wanted. I should have known better than to trust her."

Sounds like the end of a love affair, doesn't it? Well, there was little love between these two professionals, but Jennie feels she did learn something she might have learned from a failed friendship or marriage. "I realize that I've finally outgrown the kind of relationship I had with my mother," she says. "I just can't go back to having to structure my life around someone like that."

Is this really the sort of thing we're supposed to learn from our careers? Shouldn't we be developing our work skills, mastering our craft, earning more money, winning awards, getting ahead? Well, yes, if that's what we want. But unless we're hermits or lighthouse keepers, we spend our work days among living human beings, and our human relationships are the real stuff our careers are made of. It's the people we work with that make our jobs wonderful or unbearable, not the title, the salary, or the prestige. Look back on the best job you've had so far: I'm willing to bet you had a great boss, or a great group of colleagues, or both.

The writer and spiritual teacher Judith Saly once told me

that human relationships throw us together like stones in a lapidary tumbler. A lapidary tumbler, if you've never seen one, is a machine that spins like a miniature cement mixer. You throw rough, semiprecious pebbles into it and leave it running somewhere where you don't have to listen to the enormous racket the stones make knocking against one another. After quite a while—days and days—the stones become smooth and polished. The same thing happens to us at work, if we're lucky. Over the course of our careers, we get thrown against all kinds of people. It makes a lot of noise, but it also smoothes our rough edges and helps us to shine.

After spending a while in the tumbler we start to understand more about the kind of job we want to have and the kind of person we want to be in that job. If we're paying attention, we learn as much from the bad circumstances as the good ones. Jennie now knows that she needs a certain amount of autonomy to be happy, and that it's an absolute prerequisite for her. She's grown in her work to the point where she needs to run her own shop. She wouldn't have known this with such certainty if she hadn't gone through the exercise of working for a controlling boss in a suffocating corporate environment. At an earlier point in her career, she might have been able to enhance her job skills by learning to function in this very environment, but by now, she knows all she cares to know about corporate gamesmanship, and she's ready to move on.

That's the other thing about the tumbler. If you keep your wits about you while you're being slammed around, you come to recognize the signs that you've learned everything you need to learn from this particular bunch of rocks, and that it's time to think about the next phase of your professional life. I'm not saying you should leave a job you're reasonably happy in, not at all. But it's wise to heed the signals that you've outgrown the position you're in. For instance:

- Do you get a little sinking feeling when you're handed the type of project you once enjoyed tackling?
- Do you know your job so well you hardly even think about it anymore?
- Is there even a small part of you that feels your real life will begin after you retire?

Then maybe, just maybe, it's time to consider finding yourself another rock pile. You are not (I remind you) what you do. You are a worthy, conscious being who happens to be doing this particular job right now.

You may not have the flexibility of being able to change careers, or even jobs, at the moment. But why not think about what might bring you more happiness—more of a sense of completeness—in the job you're in? Could you, for example, take on some new tasks and jettison some old ones? Would your management be open to your working a four-day week? Having that extra day away from the office, if you can swing it, makes a huge difference in the rhythm of your life and helps you feel like less of a wage slave even if you're still putting in the same number of hours.

What if you're fairly satisfied with your job and schedule but you feel bored and restless all the same? What if you're not actively unhappy but not exactly happy, either? What if the days and weeks go by pleasantly enough but leave you feeling a bit dead inside?

A feeling of deadness is, pardon the expression, a dead give-away that you're not paying attention to some of your own feelings or needs. If, for example, you've told yourself you have to remain in your current job as long as your kids are in school, you've effectively put any major career change on hold—which is fine as long as some part of you isn't crying out for a major change right this minute. Even if you really do have to stay put for a while, you'll feel a lot more alive if you acknowledge the part of you that longs to be doing something different. You'll even be able to start dreaming and planning your next life while you're serving your time in this one.

A feeling of deadness can also indicate that there's some

aspect of your current job you'd rather not deal with. Let's look at Jennie's situation again. It took her very little time to realize she'd made a mistake in signing on with her current boss, because she'd made this same mistake at least once before, at the beginning of her career. Her boss back then was also controlling and untrustworthy, but Jennie was too young and inexperienced to see it. She knew only that she couldn't do anything right and that it was somehow all her fault. At the time, this was such a familiar feeling for Jennie—she'd felt this way through her entire childhood—that she fell into her childhood habit of cutting off her panic and insecurity and trying to be perfect. After about six months of this, she realized she felt absolutely joyless about her job, a job she'd really wanted. When she looked a little more closely at her situation, she realized she was actively miserable—and that's when she started looking for a way out.

In work, as in love, we tend to make the same mistakes over and over. But if we're paying attention, we make those mistakes a little less blindly, and suffer from them a little less, each time around. The first time Jennie worked for a boss who reminded her of her mother, she had to struggle to stand up for herself. Now, after years of standing up for herself and working with various types of people, she can spot a potentially tricky situation a mile away. If she gets enmeshed in a tight spot anyway, she wastes little time in extricating herself. Sounds like I'm talking about friendships or love affairs again, doesn't it?

Consider the possibility that the people you work with, the people in your particular lapidary tumbler, are hitting you in the very places you need to be hit—they're waking you up to the personal issues you most need to look at. Consider that your pursuit of vocational happiness is as personal as it is professional, in that you're seeking to grow in self-awareness and self-consciousness as much as in experience and influence. Consider that your soul-mate job, the mirror of your best self, may actually be the job you're in right now—even if it's imperfect, even if it's actively awful. Because the job you're in now, the imperfection right in front of you, is showing you what you need to face in order to *become* your best self.

. . . .

Exercise: Why This Rock Pile? Why Now?

I don't know whether you believe in karma, the idea (broadly speaking) that what goes around comes around. But it's very useful to look at your present job as a kind of karmic expression of your life so far. Try this thought experiment: Forget about why you *think* you took this job. ("It's a logical next step on my career path," or "My Uncle Lou is the chairman of the board," or "What the hell *else* was I supposed to do?") Forget what field you're in and what you expect to be doing five years from now. Focus instead on the personal issues this job brings up in the here and now—focus, in other words, on those aspects of your job that make you uncomfortable.

Look at your relationships with the people you work with, your bosses, your colleagues, your staff (if you have one):

- Is there someone you don't get along with?
- Is there someone you're pretty sure you wouldn't get along with if you didn't take elaborate precautions to stay out of his or her way?
- What are the points of friction, if any?
- Is there someone you're a little afraid of without knowing why?

Don't think too deeply about these points of friction. Just take note of them for now.

Think about your place in the pecking order:

- Is there anything about having a boss, or being a boss, that makes you uncomfortable?
- Are there people you find it difficult to confront?

- Are you sometimes too eager to please, or too inclined to be displeased?
- Are there times when you see people as bosses or underlings first and human beings second?

Once you've taken inventory of the various discomforts you experience in your work relationships, choose one specific discomfort and ask yourself, "Have I had this same feeling before in other jobs, or in my childhood?" Try to track this particular discomfort through your life, from childhood on, and observe the forms it took. Say, for example, that you have a boss who subtly puts you down while pretending to support you. Did you have a big brother who did the same thing? A teacher? A lover? Where have you encountered this emotional karma before?

....

Okay. That's it. You probably expect me to tell you that these discomforts are emotional issues that need to be tackled, problems that need to be solved. Well, your discomforts do represent important issues in your life, but you can't instantly "solve" them like algebraic equations. What you can do is observe them, and have a little compassion for yourself. You can say to yourself, "Every discomfort I encounter at work represents something my life is trying to teach me. Whenever I pay attention to a particular discomfort, I have another opportunity to bring a very old hurt into the healing light of consciousness. Just being aware of this hurt—without trying to make it go away—will ultimately help me heal it."

I mean that. The problems we face in life are not hurdles to be jumped or penances to be done. They are conditions to be embraced, conditions that teach us what we need to learn. Happiness is not a static, finite quantity, a quarry to be pursued. But we may find it in the pursuit itself—if we have compassion for our own struggle.

Mantra for the Bad Days:

It could be worse. I could be *related* to these people.

Chapter 10 The Worst That Can Happen

KEYWORD

change

I remember watching, years ago, a wildlife documentary about a herd of African elephants. Most of the details escape me, but I do remember this one old bull elephant, covered with ugly scars, who was accorded quite a bit of respect by the rest of the herd. (I forget whether he also got his pick of the females. Probably not.) This scarred old guy was the institutional memory of the herd. He'd been in the most fights and lived to tell about them. He lingered in my memory because after I'd been in the magazine business for a while, I began to feel like that beat-up elephant.

The magazine world as I knew it was small, incestuous, and volatile. Editors-in-chief and publishers were hired and fired with unnerving frequency, and every time someone in a top slot was replaced by someone else, most of the rest of the staff would turn over within about six months. There was no real job security. People shot around the industry like pinballs, trying to score higher salaries, better titles, and saner work environments. I shot around with everyone else. I remember sitting in a new-employee orientation session at one company and realizing it was the *fourth* time I'd been hired there. When I remarked on this, nobody in the room batted an eye. Ten months later, the editor who'd hired me was fired, and I quit to go someplace else.

Lest you think this lack of job security made me jumpy or pessimistic, I can reassure you: It made me serene. And fearless. It taught me that when the worst happens in a job, you always live through it, and that sometimes the worst really *is* for the best. Spending a decade sitting in a Zen monastery couldn't have taught me more about my own inner resources than playing musical chairs in the magazine business. Not that it didn't burn me out after a decade or two. But I did pick up some pearls of elephant wisdom along the way, which I'll share as concisely as I can. So go ahead: Read my scars.

⦿ Pearl 1: A Bad Boss Is Your Teacher

Never your favorite teacher. But often an important teacher. As I've said, there are many kinds of bad bosses, but you always know them when you report to them. For the purposes of this discussion, a bad boss is a boss who's bad *for you*—one who

makes you feel undermined, undervalued, insecure, chronically
angry, or just plain bad. No boss is universally bad. The worst
boss I ever had was loved, or at least liked, by some of her
staff—and I thought she was the incarnation of evil. (I still do,
but somebody must like her, because she's still pulling down
seven figures.)

No, I take that back. Some bosses *are* universally bad. Ed,
an engineer I know, once had a boss who tormented everybody
whose path he crossed. This guy, whom I'll call Ray, wasn't
just irrational, he was pathological; his wife ultimately tried to
enlist Ed's help in having him committed. Ray was the kind of
bad boss who lures you into a job by telling you how much he
needs you, then sabotages you at every turn. He made Ed's life
a living hell. He'd torture him all day, then he'd call him at
home and torture him some more. After about eight months,
Ray fired Ed, then gave him a bad reference that kept him from
getting hired someplace else. It took Ed six months to land
another job, during which time he ran out of money and nearly
lost his house. It was, by any standard, a low point in his life.

Ed still shivers involuntarily when he remembers this inter-
lude, but he admits he learned some valuable lessons from it
(besides the obvious lesson that if you're working for a psycho,
it's a bad idea to list him as a job reference). For one thing, he

learned to heed his own gut. "When you're interviewing for a job, you tend to say what you think they want to hear," he says. "If I hadn't been so intent on presenting myself in a good light, I might have listened a little harder and picked up on this guy's weird intensity." Ed also learned that there are some people who simply can't be pleased. This may not sound like much of a lesson to you, but to Ed, who had always bent over backward to please the authority figures in his life, it came as a revelation. "I've always been the type who responds to a difficult boss by trying harder," he says. "But with Ray, I finally realized that pleasing the boss is not the point. Doing my best work is the point." Ah: Enlightenment.

Working for a bad boss points you in the direction of a truth you need to acquire. Often this truth has something to do with learning to value yourself. Think about it: When you're working for a person who makes you feel bad about yourself in some way, the real challenge is to get your self-esteem back. So the question to ask is not, "Why is this bozo torturing me?" but "*How* is this bozo torturing me? How, exactly, is he or she challenging my sense of self-worth—and what can I do about it?"

There is always something you can do about it. Maybe you need to have a talk with your boss, or with someone in Human Resources. Maybe you need to ask yourself whether you're trying too hard to please. Maybe you need to look for another job. Or maybe you just need to say to yourself, "Hey, wait a minute—I'm worth *more* than this. I don't *deserve* to be treated badly!" This is a magnificently subversive statement, even if nobody hears it but you.

My elephant guarantee: You can never go wrong if you ask yourself, "Why have I crossed paths with this boss? Why now? What is this experience trying to teach me?"

Pearl 2: Everybody Should Be Fired at Least Once in Their Career

Yes, I've been fired, early in my career, from a job I probably shouldn't have accepted in the first place, as a press agent for classical musicians. This seemed like a logical position for me, especially since I already had experience as a publicist, but my boss, who had promised to show me the ropes, gave me no direction whatever and generally treated me as though I was an enormous disappointment to her. I had zero, count 'em, zero good days in that office before she gave me the boot. (Later she tried to hire me back at a reduced salary. I said no.)

I was mortified. I had never considered myself the sort of person who gets fired, whatever that means, and despite the fact that I hadn't liked the job, I didn't want to think of myself as having failed at it. Now I was not only jobless, I was also clueless about what to do next. So I vamped for a while, as they say in the music business. I did freelance publicity work to pay the rent, and knocked at a bunch of doors to see if any would open. Several months later, a door opened in the magazine business.

Stop yawning. Of course a door opened; some door always opens sooner or later. The interesting thing about this episode was that being fired was not the end of the world. Somehow, I'd thought it would be. Granted, I was young and naïve, but I'd really thought being fired conferred some kind of indelible mark of shame. In fact, it turned out that practically everyone I knew had been fired from some job or other, and they'd all experienced the same strange mixture of trauma and relief. Furthermore, they'd all eventually found their way to better jobs than the ones they'd left—better emotionally if not financially. Being fired, I learned, is like a scientific experiment that doesn't work: You look at the data, try to figure out where you went wrong, and use what you've learned to set up the next experiment.

Being fired is never easy; sometimes it's harrowing. But it teaches you that you can lose a job ignominiously and survive—and I can't tell you what a valuable piece of experience that is.

My elephant guarantee: Once you live through the worst career trauma that could possibly happen to you—whatever you think that is—you learn that it, too, passes eventually. Letting it happen is the same thing as letting it go.

🍐 Pearl 3: The Good Times Never Last, but Neither Do the Bad Times

If you've ever studied Buddhism, you're familiar with the idea that unhappiness arises from our constant effort to cling to pleasure and push away pain. We want the beautiful moments in our lives to last forever, and become anxious that they won't last. They never last. We also devote a great deal of energy to avoiding unpleasantness, which is impossible.

I bring this up because there inevitably come points in a working person's life when good job situations turn sour for one reason or another. As I said in chapter 5, this often happens when a bad boss replaces a good one. But it can also happen when a faltering economy undermines what used to be a flourishing business, when a well-functioning team breaks up, or when you outgrow the position you're in.

I've had several jobs where I was part of a really good team, where my colleagues and I liked and respected each other and derived active pleasure from working together. The first time one of these teams broke up, when a new boss came in and reorganized the department, I was indignant. We'd all been doing good work, and I didn't see why the fun had to end. So I was, to put it charitably, resistant to the new regime, because I felt personally wronged by it. As a result, I stayed angry a lot longer than I needed to.

Well, as I said, I was in a volatile industry. By the third or fourth time I worked on a great team that got dismantled by a new boss, I was much more philosophical. I had learned that a good team is a rare and precious thing with a finite life span, so you'd better enjoy it while you've got it. I'd also learned that the tough times in one's career—difficult transitions, down-turns, layoffs, management idiocies—also have finite life spans. You live through them and learn from them. Tough times, too, become your teachers.

My elephant guarantee: It's immensely liberating to accept the fact that sometimes your job is awful and sometimes it's won-derful. The bad times aren't nearly as bad if you can envision an end to them, and the good times are that much more pre-cious if you know they can't last.

Exercise: Riding the Waves of Change

By this time I'm sure you've realized that I'm not really talking about bad job experiences happening to good people. I'm talking about the inevitability of change, and our resistance to it. Good times and bad times tend to come in waves, and it's much easier to ride those waves than it is to struggle against them.

I'd like you to think of three good things about your present work situation. (Come on, I *know* you can come up with three of them.) Perhaps there's somebody you enjoy working with, or for. Maybe you're involved with a project you find really interesting. Or you like the view from your office window. Whatever these three positive things are, take a few minutes to focus on your good feelings about them. I'm asking you to enjoy them. And be grateful for them.

Now introduce the idea that none of these circumstances can possibly last. Don't dramatize it; just remind yourself that you won't always be working for this great boss, or that the fabulous project will have to come to an end, or that you won't have this view forever. How does this make you feel?

I know that when I picture something that makes me happy, I get a little stab of anxiety when I realize this happiness is finite and transitory—transitory as all get out. The people I love are going to die, and so am I. Even our experience of love—immortal love—must change as our lives and bodies change. There is simply no way to grab happiness and fix it in place. So why not let go of it? Why not just enjoy the gifts of the moment and be grateful for them in the moment? Mind you, it's not easy. But I'd like you to try.

Think of the snowdrops' brief moment in February, the fireflies that flourish so alarmingly for a mere three weeks in July, or the first apple cider of September, pressed from Macintoshes and clear as a bell. Half the joy of these events is in their transitory nature: They're here, and then they're gone. We try to be there to experience them; it's the best we can do.

There's a second half to this exercise. Think of three *negative* things about your present work situation. I suspect I don't have to coach you to come up with these. Maybe you've got a bad boss, or a strained relationship with a colleague or client. Maybe you're underpaid and unhappy about it, or you have more work than you can handle. Anyhow, think about these negative things. Now remind yourself that these circumstances are trying to teach you something—about yourself, about life. This is important. As I said, bad times are your teachers, and figuring out what the lesson is can help you get through them in one piece.

· ·

You *will* get through the bad times, because they, too, are finite and transitory. Look, I'm not trying to be Pollyanna, here. Some circumstances are genuinely tough, and they don't seem transitory. If you lose a leg, you're not going to grow it back. But your feelings about your situation will change as you learn to cope and gradually regain your confidence. Some kind of wholeness will return to you even if the limb won't.

Please believe this. If you can't hold onto happiness, you can't hold onto unhappiness either. And you are still you, whether you're living through the best of times or the worst of times.

Mantra for the Bad Days:

This idiocy, too, shall pass.

Chapter 11　My Cubicle, My Chapel

If you think I'm about to tell you how to create your own altar at work, you've bought the wrong book. It's hard enough to create a sense of personal space at the office, let alone sacred space. But of course, you need both, which means you have to define both for yourself. It's not easy.

Looking back on my many jobs, I realize I've rarely had anything resembling the office space of my dreams, that small, spare sanctuary with a window and a door and adequate ventilation, situated just far enough from office traffic so I could be part of the flow of business without feeling inundated by it—so I could be in the working world but not *of* the working world. Sounds like a reasonable, not-too-greedy wish, doesn't it? I've often visualized myself working in such a space, since visualization is supposed to help you create what you want. (Right?)

Well, it hasn't helped much. You should see the offices I've had: cubicles and half cubicles covered in dingy beige fabric. Battered, tired furniture that looked as though it harbored decades' worth of germs. Evil fluorescent lighting that hummed as it went about its work of making everyone look deathly ill. Carpeting whose intrinsic ugliness was little improved by trodden-in grime. You know places like that; you've probably worked in them.

I'm not saying you need a beautiful office to remind you that you have a beautiful soul. But it doesn't hurt. And being cast into some bleak, dingy corner right next to the copying machine sure doesn't help. Maybe if I were truly evolved (whatever that means), I'd be able to function blissfully in an ugly, unwelcoming office space, but I can't. Bureaucratic bleakness eats away at the soul.

I once thought that as I moved into better jobs I'd get better office space, but this has not been the case. Perhaps this is because I've worked in New York City, where light and space are at a premium, or because I'm a writer and editor by trade rather than, say, a corporate lawyer. Perhaps I just have bad office karma. But I usually have the kind of space I'm embarrassed to bring friends to, the kind where plants die.

I used to ask myself: Shouldn't people's office spaces be some sort of outpicturing of their inner selves? Shouldn't we be able to create workspaces that enable us to give our best selves to our jobs? And (I couldn't help asking) if our offices do indeed reveal something about our inner selves, what on earth is wrong with me?

For a couple of years I was lucky enough to work at *Glamour* under the legendary editor Ruth Whitney. We had the best, deepest staff in the magazine business, and the resources to make every story as good as it possibly could be. (This, I should explain, is a rarity in magazines, where staffs are often small, budgets are tight, and you're lucky if you can crank out stories that are good *enough*.) Unfortunately, we also had the lousiest office space in the business. High-level editors were jammed—in pairs—into cubicles or former closets. Hardly anybody had real walls, let alone doors. Though I had an exalted title, I shared a cubicle in the articles department, where I was surrounded by editors who talked on the phone with writers all day. I could hear everybody's conversations and they could hear mine, a circumstance which made me feel naked and paranoid, and which made it remarkably difficult to write or think.

Over time, I found I could tune out the noise and summon the concentration to write when I had to, though it was never easy. The thing I couldn't tune out was my own resentment: *A woman in my position, with my salary,* I thought, *should not have to share a goddamn cubicle*. My resentment was part of the *Glamour* culture in those days. We were an overlarge, overqualified staff, collegial yet competitive. Ruth wanted us lean and hungry and fighting, cordially, for space—in the office and in the magazine. She also wanted us listening to and learning from each other. Ruth herself seemed to have no need for personal space; she actually shared her office with an assistant. Have I mentioned that I loved working for her? I did, even when I wasn't speaking to her.

My point is that far from reflecting our deeper selves, our offices actually reflect the culture of our workplace, politics and all. The things we dislike about our office space are a concrete representation of the things we dislike about that culture. Do you work for a company that parcels out windows as though they were diamonds? That doesn't vacuum without a court order? That willfully misunderstands the meaning of the word "privacy"? That discourages the display of personal photos or art? That reminds you in endless ways that you're on their turf, not yours?

Well, you *are* on their turf. And even if your firm makes reasonable accommodations for employees' individuality, you are probably expected to check part of your identity at the door, the better to meld with the corporate mission. You work under their roof; you follow their rules. It's like living in your parents' house all over again, except that you don't get to run into your room and slam the door, and you absolutely don't get to play heavy metal at top volume.

I invoke this metaphor deliberately. As I've already pointed out, there's a good deal of parent-child stuff going on in the average workplace. Companies often style themselves as "families," a term that has to ring false since they are, after all, paying you to show up. You're expected to sign on to your company's ideals, or at least its way of doing business. And unless you're in top management, you're given very little control over your work space. The office you're assigned is the literal, physical expression of your firm's authority over you. If they stick you in a cubicle—even if they stick *everybody* into cubicles—it's hard not to take it personally. *What do I have to do to rate four lousy walls and my own ceiling? Haven't I come farther than this in life?*

Realistically or not, we tend to perceive our space as a measure of the company's appreciation of us, or of our own success. And our perception changes with our moods and circumstances. Sometimes I actually felt a sort of gritty pride about working in my *Glamour* cubicle: *I don't care what my sur-*

roundings look like as long as I'm doing good work. But some days the place felt like a prison cell: *Is this how I really want to spend my life?*

Ups and downs like these are normal; the trick is to experience them mindfully rather than mindlessly. If you become aware of your day-to-day reactions to your office space, you become a lot more conscious of where you stand with your job—how much resistance you have to it, how much pleasure you derive from it, how challenged or bored you are. If you let your feelings about your space remain unconscious, they become part of the general background noise: At best, they sap your energy; at worst, they become part of your personal Slough of Suckiness.

Looked at this way, your workspace *is* an outpicturing of your inner self, in that it gives you a reliable barometer of your relationship to your job. Being aware of yourself in your physical space is, after all, a form of meditation. And as with all meditation, awareness itself is the point, not instant happiness, and not coming to any grand conclusions about what you're supposed to be doing with your life.

Exercise: Making Your Work Space a Sacred Space

I'm still not going to tell you how to build an altar at your desk. I have nothing against altars, but if I had one of my own, I certainly wouldn't want it in my office. I do, however, believe that your office can feel like a sacred space at least some of the time, by virtue of your own conscious presence in it. It may be the cubicle from hell, but you occupy it, and you bring your divinity there with you.

To begin to feel—how should I put this?—the sacred potential of your workspace, you need to make a small commitment to noticing your response to it. By "small commitment," I mean you need to make only a small effort, but you need to make it at least once a day. First thing in the morning is a good time: When you arrive at your office and open the door (assuming you have a door), turn on the light, and take off your coat, simply take note of how you feel about this place in this moment. Note how your body feels. How do the quality of the air, the quality of the light, the sound (maybe) of the light fixture affect you physically? How does the space itself affect you—does it make you feel hemmed in? Expansive? What about the noise level? Do you feel peaceful? Jangled?

Become aware, too, of how the place makes you feel emotion-ally. Do you feel ready to get to work, or does your heart sink a little? Or a lot? Does the sight of the place awaken any festering resentments toward management? (such as: *Those cheap bastards won't even pay to have the carpet cleaned!*) Are there certain resentments you tend to have every time you really look at your surroundings? Take note of them. I'm not suggesting you delve deeply into these resentments. I'm simply suggesting that you become aware of them. Notice your feelings, whatever they are; then let them go. If your lack of a door or window brings up anger or frustration, simply note it objectively, without letting yourself wallow in it. Say to yourself: Here I am, and this is how I feel at this moment.

Repeat this little exercise from time to time throughout the day. What you're doing is taking a few moments to check in with your body, to be in the room you're in, and to note what it feels like to be in that room. I've found that these "Here I am" moments are very useful for reminding myself that I am more than my job, and that my reality is greater than the physical space I happen to be sitting in and grousing about. These moments are actually centering exercises, and anything that makes you feel more centered invites the sacred into your space.

This is all very practical, but (I hear you ask) isn't there a more active way to make your physical office space feel sacred? Well, yes. For one thing, you can modulate your own speaking voice. Pay attention to the way you sound when you're on the phone or speaking in person to a colleague. What would happen if you made a conscious effort to make your voice as pleasing as possible—to shape your words with care, to respect both speaker and listener by bringing your full attention to the sounds you're making? The quality of those sounds will affect the quality of the silence around them, infusing your space with joy or deadness, reverence or raucousness. You might think this is completely nuts, but sometimes the most beautiful thing about a space is the person in it: beauty of thought, beauty of sound, beauty of word, beauty of intent. And yes, you can pray if you're so inclined (see "Working and Praying," page 70).

You might also want to keep some sort of personal talisman around. Choose an object that has some kind of spiritual meaning for you and keep it in an unobtrusive place—in your desk drawer if necessary. I'm not talking about religious images that call overt attention to your beliefs. These, in my opinion, do not belong in a communal secular workplace, and displaying them may actually run counter to company policy. I'm talking about small objects that somehow remind you who you are.

For example, I always keep stones around me because I find them centering and comforting. People mistake them for décor, but they're not; they're my sanity in tangible form. In one office, I kept a basket of rounded granite beach stones behind the door. They came from Block Island, a place where I feel at peace.

Nestled in my computer keyboard was a cat's-eye moonstone my husband had given me. Tucked away in a drawer, where I could reach for it in moments of panic, was a lump of green amber.

After a while, though, the stone population got out of control. I had to group them in baskets to get them out of the way: lumps of labradorite and chrysoprase; garnet and aquamarine crystals; jade, lapis, hematite, pyrite, rose quartz, ruby zoisite, and bloodstone. Among others. This was a particularly stressful job, and, okay, I *do* have altar-building tendencies.

Which brings me to my final point: Sacred talismans are all very well, but there's only so much stress they can absorb. There are times when the most spiritual thing you can do in your office is to leave it and shut the door behind you, taking your sacred space with you—even if it's only for a few minutes. Pay attention, and you'll know when those times are.

Mantra for the Bad Days:

If God had wanted me to spend my whole life in my office,

He would have given me a nicer office.

Chapter 12

Who's Cracking the Whip?

········ KEYWORD ········

good

Katherine just called me to cancel our lunch date. I'd been looking forward to seeing her, and God knows I could use a break from work, but I should have known better than to get my hopes up—Katherine cancels more lunch dates than she keeps. We've already rescheduled this one twice. She has an impeccable excuse, as usual: "I've spent the past three weeks working on a new batch of fabric patterns"—Katherine is a designer for a textile company—"and my boss hates *everything* I've done! She says I've got it all wrong, she wants it to feel more Tibetan and my stuff is too Chinese. So I have to go down to the library and do more research on Tibetan iconography, and I just can't take time to have lunch. I'm *sooooo* sorry!"

Katherine always apologizes charmingly. She really is sorry to wimp out on me, but she's overworked and a perfectionist; she has tight deadlines and an arbitrary, unpleaseable boss.

This is why I rarely see her over a lunch table or even a dinner table. She wants to give her best to the job. I understand. The problem is that she'd also like to give her best to the *rest* of her life—her friends, her hobbies, her love life—but she allows her job to eat up the lion's share of her time and energy. She's aware that her schedule is seriously out of balance, but she can't see a way to fix it. She's a dedicated professional. She's also a doormat.

Katherine is self-aware enough to know there are two sides to her dedication. One side, obviously, is that she's good at what she does and serious about earning her paycheck. The other side is that she doesn't have the nerve to stand up to her boss. In fact, she irrationally believes she's in danger of being fired if she doesn't produce twice as much work as anyone else. In trying to be a good worker, she's acting more like a good little girl.

Let's take a brief time out to look at that adjective "good." We use it so often we rarely stop to think about what we mean by it. Katherine, for example, wants to be a "good" worker (dedicated, productive, capable), a "good" person (ethical, kind, understanding), and a "good" colleague (supportive, cooperative, generous). These are all, from a spiritual point of view, desirable things. But she sometimes tries so hard to live up to her own image of being "good" that she stops enjoying her work and starts feeling oppressed by it. The tasks that once interested her become a compulsion: Gotta meet the deadline. Can't have lunch. Can't have a life.

We all go into that compulsive mode sometimes, and it can be exhilarating to see how much work we produce under pressure. The question we need to ask ourselves is: Who's cracking the whip? Are we driving ourselves for the joy of it, the sheer adrenaline rush? Are we being driven by an external authority, or by our own fear of not measuring up? Or is it some combination of the two, as in Katherine's case?

Katherine basically likes the task at hand. She loves having an excuse to research Tibetan iconography, or anything else for that matter. Gathering images and filtering them through her artist's brain is exciting and stimulating for her; it makes her itch to sit down and draw, the other thing she loves most in the world. But then comes the hard part: getting her designs approved by her boss, Carrie, who can be counted upon to reject at least half of Katherine's work for no discernible reason. Katherine is used to arbitrary rejection. Her mother was impossible to please, and so was her favorite art professor in college. She has come to believe, unconsciously, that being rejected is part of being "good," both as an artist and as a person. She doesn't want to know how angry she is at Carrie and her mother and the other rejecting women in her life, because being angry is *not* part of being "good." Rather than feel her anger, in fact, she works harder. Voilà! A highly productive doormat is born.

As I said, Katherine is reasonably self-aware, and she knows she should be doing something to take charge of her schedule, because spending long hours at her job—her "good" job—is beginning to make her miserable. She's just not sure *what* she should do. Go into therapy to explore her anger at her mom and her need for approval? Maybe; it might help in the long run. Go into a screaming fit and tell Carrie to stick her rapidograph where the sun don't shine? Probably not. Quit her job and go into her own design business? Possibly, if she's burning to become an entrepreneur.

But going into therapy and starting her own business are long-term solutions. What can Katherine do in the moment she's in right now? For starters, she can *be* in that moment. She can notice how she feels about canceling her lunch date with me. She can notice how she feels about having another batch of designs rejected. She can notice her pleasure in doing research. She can notice her anxiety at having to hurry twice as hard to make her deadline.

There is a vast difference between simply being swept up in the frenzy of a task and *noticing* that you're being swept up in it. In the latter case, you become aware of the *quality* of the frenzy—you notice whether you're anxious or angry or exhilarated or all the above. That's when you can ask yourself: "Who's cracking the whip?" and notice the answer. You can also notice a whole bunch of other useful stuff, such as, "I'm hungry. I need to eat something." Or "I'm too tired to think straight. I need to go home." Or "I'm too angry to think straight. I need to walk around the block." Or "I'm incredibly good at this—how wonderful!" The very act of observing these things puts you in the driver's seat—the driver's seat of consciousness, where you get to be in your own body and have your own feelings and give yourself what you need in the moment.

If Katherine learns to notice what she's feeling in the frenzy of the moment, she'll still, probably, be inclined to work too hard, but she'll be able to make a more conscious choice to do so. She'll still have to deal with her rejecting boss, but she'll become more aware of the pluses and minuses of working for said boss, and of her own choice to stay in this job or seek a new one. Most important, by noticing the moments of genuine pleasure in her work, she'll become more connected to that pleasure. She'll know how "good" she is at her work—and that can only make her stronger.

Her alternative is to keep working too hard and keep resenting it, and then, perhaps, to burn out—to reach a point where she takes little or no pleasure in her work and starts to feel dead inside. Feeling dead inside may be a sign of exhaustion, but it's also, as I've said, a pretty reliable sign that you're cutting off some feeling or set of feelings. Katherine, for instance, has become accustomed to suppressing her anger because she's afraid of that perfectly human aspect of herself. There's a good deal of energy in anger, energy that could help motivate Katherine to find creative solutions to her job dilemma. But first, she has to give herself permission to feel it—not all at once in a murderous rush, but moment by moment, as it speaks in her soul.

Being a good person, a good worker, a good colleague does not mean being totally infallible, unflappable, or unstinting. It means bringing your whole human self to work, dark side and all. No job is perfect and no human being is perfect (*there's* a newsflash). So the only control you really have is to acknowledge, even embrace, your own day-to-day struggle—there's honor in that struggle—and to commit yourself to doing the best you can on any given day.

Let me put it another way: If you bring your evil twin to work, maybe you'll accomplish twice as much.

· ·

Exercise: How "Good" Are You at Your Job?

It's Blue Sky time. Describe the person you'd *like* to be at work—the ideal you'd live up to if you were a perfectly realized being in a perfect world. I, for example, would be endlessly cheerful and creative, able to come up with astonishing ideas and execute them in virtuoso ways that would leave my colleagues breathless. I'd be funny yet nurturing, making the people around me feel valued and optimistic. I would begin every day with a little centering prayer and stay focused on the task in front of me. I'd work hard enough to feel virtuous but not exploited. I'd be the most productive person on the staff, but nobody would resent me for it. I'd never, ever, say a negative word about anybody, except for those few people in every industry who are so obviously evil they really beg to be badmouthed. Oh, and I'd have better clothes than I have now.

You get the idea. Describe the best worker you can imagine being—you, but better. Include the characteristics that are most important to you, whether they have to do with the job itself, the way you feel about it, or the way you interact with your colleagues. Write those characteristics down, or just think about them in a focused way. What are the traits you value most in yourself? How would you like to see yourself expressing those traits in the working world? What, in short, is your idea of being *good*?

How attainable do you believe this ideal self is? Is there part of you that believes you really could live up to it if you just kept trying? Because you *can't* live up to it—not 100 percent of the time, anyway. As I'm sure you know perfectly well, there will be days when you're brilliant, and days when you can't even get out of bed right.

Now switch gears. Describe the *worst* worker you know how to be. Imagine what would happen if you allowed your basest impulses to spill out into the world like so much bilge. I, for example, would show up late, spend as much time as possible on personal phone calls, make my assistant run personal errands for me, and take long expense-account lunches. I would justify this by telling myself and anyone else who'd listen that my job was total bullshit and that the company was being run by idiots. I'd recycle the same ideas over and over while feeling contempt for management which, after all, only *wants* the same old stuff over and over. I would make it known to all and sundry that work was hell and I was only in it for the paycheck—which, by the way, wasn't enough. Oh, and I'd have better clothes than I have now.

Again, you get the drift. What's your idea of being bad? Is there part of you that believes you'd actually be this bad if you gave yourself half a chance?

....

I submit to you—humbly or arrogantly, depending on whether I'm being a good girl or a bad girl—that you probably express aspects of *both* your best and worst selves all the time. You can probably find reasons to be both proud and ashamed of yourself on any given day. Furthermore, if you look closely at these two selves, you'll see that both are equally unrealistic: One's unrealistically good, the other unrealistically bad. But it's instructive to get to know them. When you find that you're working too hard and resenting it, it's probably one of these two selves who's cracking the whip. You're either striving to be impossibly good, or striving to avoid being impossibly bad.

Well, just stop it. As James Thurber so brilliantly put it, you might as well fall flat on your face as lean over too far backward. It's enough—more than enough—to be aware of the best and the worst in you, and to be as good as you can manage to be in the moment at hand. Remember: Every aspect of you contains energy, even if some of that energy is temporarily tied up in a negative feeling or belief. You need the whole mixed bag of it. Get to know it all.

Mantra for the Bad Days:

I'm the one who's cracking the whip—so nobody's going to notice if I stop.

Burnout

When you pit a human being, in a physical body, against an overwhelming workload, something has to give, and it isn't the workload. No matter how "evolved" we are, no matter how dedicated to our work, sometimes the deck really is stacked against us. Some jobs are structured to burn us out, and *will* burn us out sooner or later. Sometimes we burn ourselves out for reasons of our own. Either way, burnout—that souldeadening mix of exhaustion and joylessness—has become a fact of working life.

It will probably not be news to you that Americans are working harder and longer than ever. Research shows that we're putting in more hours than we used to, yet we still feel we don't have time to get everything done. Our jobs follow us home in the form of faxes and e-mails, eating into our time with our families—and if you raise children, you know that's more than a full-time job in itself. We are, as a country, over-worked, underrested, and dangerously stressed out.

I write this in the midst of a recession, when staffs and budg-ets are being slashed and those employees who don't get laid off are being asked to absorb the extra work and be grateful they still have jobs. But I can also remember, without trying very hard, boom times when businesses were expanding so fast we all had more work than we could handle. There are always real, compelling reasons to work harder than we want to or should. There are always real, compelling reasons to let our jobs take over our lives. And there are often unfair circum-stances—stacked decks—that turn our jobs into soul killers.

This is why, when I'm rash enough to bring up the subject of spirituality in the workplace, people tend to stare at me incred-ulously and say, "*What* spirituality?" In the average workplace, to all appearances, there just plain isn't any.

So here's my question: How do we keep from losing our spiritual shirts in jobs that are burning us out? Without sugar-coating the harsh realities of the working world, without deny-ing that we're sometimes asked to carry more weight than we can bear, how can we do our jobs conscientiously and emerge with our bodies and souls intact?

Part of the answer, I think, is to keep our eyes on the spiritual prize, i.e., to be mindful of the things we find rewarding about our jobs. My neighbor Ellen, for example, is a prime candidate for burnout. To hear her talk about her work, you'd think she was already going down in flames—except that there's a lightness of spirit about her, a resilience that's apparent even when she's discouraged and dead tired. Ellen is a high school teacher, one of the passionate, dynamic ones. She's been teaching for over 30 years, and it's obvious she's still crazy about her work. In fact, she can't imagine doing anything else. What I find remarkable is that she feels this way in a job that regularly drives her to tears of frustration and exhaustion.

Ellen feels hampered by having to follow a curriculum designed around mandatory state-run tests; it swamps her in paperwork and leaves her little room for creativity. Most of the time she regards this as a challenge. She likes coming up with new ways to engage her students' minds while stuffing every bit of required knowledge into them. It's the kids' parents that really make her job hard: They're angry at the school system, and Ellen has to bear the brunt of it. "Day after day I get yelled at for not doing enough to make sure their children do their homework or pass their tests," she says. "One mother screamed at me for not telling her that her son wasn't handing in his homework. I asked if she was monitoring his assignment sheets, and she told me he wouldn't let her look in his backpack. She was reluctant to take responsibility for parenting him, in other words, so it became *my* responsibility.

"I'm a civil servant. I work for these parents. I understand I'm in charge of their precious children. It's simply not appropriate for me to get angry back at them, so I just stand there and take it. Then I go home and cry. And *then* I do the three hours worth of paperwork I haven't had time for because I've been listening to parents yell at me."

Ellen won't speculate on why the parents are so angry. I wonder whether it's because they, too, have jobs that leave them overworked and exhausted. Maybe they're frustrated because they lack the time and energy to monitor their kids, who in turn face an incredibly competitive struggle to get into college. Whatever the reason, every teacher Ellen knows has to cope with the same problem. "It's especially hard for the younger ones, who lack the experience not to take it personally," she says. "I'm glad I'm close to retirement. The situation seems to be getting worse and worse." Then she pauses and says, "But I'll probably go right back into teaching after a year or two. I just love it so much!"

Ah—the L Word. Love may not conquer all, but it sure helps to shore you up through an endless workday. If Ellen is burning out, she's at least doing it in a job she loves, so the positive aspects of her work tend to balance out the negative ones. Even though the reality of teaching doesn't come close to matching her shining vision of it, she believes that her work matters, and that she's giving it her best shot, fighting the good fight. She still feels connected to the sense of deeper purpose that drew her toward this career in the first place. Well, not all of us are so lucky.

What if you're in a job that's burning you out without the benefit of a sense of deeper purpose? What if your workload is just plain crushing and not even a little bit rewarding? What could be remotely spiritual about that?

At the risk of overtaxing a metaphor, I will remind you that the same fire that burns can also anneal, or strengthen. A certain amount of burnout can be a tempering experience in a working person's life. It can show you your strengths. It can show you your limits. And—perhaps most important—it can teach you to respect those limits, to take care of yourself, to stand up for yourself when no one else will.

Please understand: I am *not* saying that burnout is noble or desirable. I'm saying it's a risk we all run, and harrowing as it is, it can have its instructive side. It forces you to ask yourself certain questions you might not ask otherwise, such as: How much can I take, anyway? Do I believe that pushing myself till I drop is some kind of virtue? What, exactly, am I trying to prove by working so hard?

And: How much of my strength and energy do I really owe my employer? How much of it belongs to me—and how do I claim it as my own?

Okay, that last one was a trick question. *All* of your strength and energy belongs to you. Believe it or not, if your job is burning you out, you're the one who's choosing to let it do so. Your employers, unless they're complete idiots, do *not* want you to crash and burn. It's not cost effective, for one thing. Say you drive yourself so hard you deplete your immune system and catch every bug that comes along: That's a drain on productivity. Say you become so exhausted you get seriously ill: That drives up their insurance costs. Say you become so disaffected you up and quit: That puts them to the considerable expense of replacing you.

What you really owe your employer is the same thing you owe yourself: The presence of mind to know when you've taken on more than you can handle, and the self-respect to work only as hard as you can and no harder.

Let's look a little more closely at Ellen's case. Not only does she love her work, she's basically an upbeat person, and that, admittedly, helps a lot. But she also has a remarkably clear view of her situation—and this clarity, I believe, is what keeps her from flaming out entirely. Ellen is not a masochist. She knows how tough her job is; she sees how the bureaucratic deck is stacked against her. But she also knows her own physical and emotional limitations—she knows when she needs to go home and sleep, and when she needs to vent her anger to a friend. Her retirement, she says, won't come a day too soon. But until that day, she's going to keep trying to come up with new ways to reach both her students and their parents. This, after all, is her job.

Seeing your job clearly, knowing both how bad and how good it is, is the kind of truth that can set you free—free to assess the situation at any given moment, and to balance your own needs with the demands of your job in that moment. This in itself is a spiritual approach to work, whether you love your job, hate your job, or go both ways about it.

. . . .

Exercise: Saying No to Burnout

You can't say no to burnout if you're already burnt out. So the first thing you have to do is check whether your pilot light is still lit. I'm not being as coy as I sound here. When a job has well and truly burnt you out, you feel dead and empty inside, with not a trace of joy in your work. And you need some amount of joy to function, even if it's the sidewise joy of being conscientious, efficient, or productive rather than joy in the job itself. You also, obviously, need a certain amount of physical energy. If you're dragging yourself through every minute of every day, you're out of fuel.

Observe yourself over the next work week with two basic questions in mind: "Where's my joy?" and "What's my energy level?" Don't get obsessive about this, just be conscious of these two things. Become aware of whatever joy you take in the job, even if it's the joy of the coffee and Danish you scarf down at your desk, or the joy of interacting with a colleague or client you like. Become aware, too, of your energy cycles during the day. How tired are you? Is the tiredness skin-deep, bone-deep, or soul-deep? Under what circumstances, if any, do you feel a little zing of energy? If you don't feel that zing until you're putting your coat on at night, you may be okay physically but burnt out emotionally, so pay attention to what happens to your energy level once you leave the office.

If you observe yourself for a week and find your pilot light is not out yet, that you still have some energy and joy left, sit down and add up your current workload. Sum up the things you have to do over the next week, month, or year, and imagine the cumulative weight of those tasks. Pretty overwhelming, right? What happens to your energy and joy when you consider your entire workload at once? Is this a familiar feeling?

When we're saddled with more work than we can handle, the burden of that workload becomes a looming presence in our lives. We have a tendency to shoulder it all at once, and this tendency, I submit, is a major factor in burnout: While we're attending to one task, we're thinking about the others lined up behind it. No matter how much we get done, we can't forget how much we still have left to do. This, by the way, is as true at home as it is at work; I'm sure you have the same endless list of household chores I have.

Now ask yourself a truly subversive question: "What would happen if I did just one task at a time, without worrying about any of the other tasks waiting to get done?" I know what you're thinking. I've read all the magazine articles—hell, I've *edited* some of them—about how we need to be "multitaskers" in order to balance our complicated lives. And in fact, I often find myself doing more than one thing at a time. But whenever I do too much multitasking (what a dreadful word), I start to feel tired and distracted and scattered. I forget who I am and become my workload; I lose my joy. The antidote is always to do the task in front of me and only that task. If I want to be truly present, one thing at a time is all I *can* do.

Don't take my word for it. Experiment for yourself: Try focusing on one blessed thing at a time, even if dozens of other things are clamoring for your attention. Keep checking in with your little pilot light. When it's out, or in danger of going out, simply stop pushing yourself. If this involves leaving a project unfinished at deadline, find a way to get help. If you have to finish the job anyway, promise yourself a break immediately afterward, and keep that promise. (This is important. If you renege on your promise to yourself, you're becoming your own slave driver.) I'm guessing, though, that on any given project, you can probably take more breaks than you think.

If, in doing this exercise, you observe that you are truly exhausted, depleted, and joyless, get yourself some rest. Immediately. Do Not Pass Go. Take some vacation time or call in sick for a week—and stop shaking your head at me and saying you just can't get away right now. If you got hit by a bus or had a death in your family, you could get away right now. Consider your current situation—your indisposition of body and soul—equally urgent. You're not in any condition to think straight, let alone figure out how to get your joy back. Give yourself a little time to replenish.

You're still shaking your head. This is what I mean when I say you may be choosing to let yourself burn out. Even if your big project is due or you have to work two jobs to put your kids through school, you're still equipped with only one body and one soul, the care of which are in your keeping. Only you can give yourself a rest when you really need one. And ultimately, the only one who's driving you is you.

> **Mantra for the Bad Days:**
> What does not kill me makes me stronger—so I'd better not let this kill me.

Chapter 14 The Goddess of Distraction

• • • • • • KEYWORDS • • • • • •

distraction ■ focus

Eleven o'clock on a Monday morning. I'm just easing into the work of the week, having lingered over breakfast, read and answered my e-mails, surfed the Net a bit, made two or three phone calls I had put off last week, and generally tried, with little success, to psych myself into doing the work I am ostensibly being paid to do. Finally, I reach a point where I can't stall any longer. I open the computer file I'm supposed to be working on, focus my attention, think half a coherent thought—and then the phone rings.

I know who it is before I even answer. It's my friend Sybil, who has a gift for calling at the very moment I'm sitting down to a task I don't want to do. Just when I've talked myself into tackling it, there she is, beguiling me into thinking about something, anything, more pleasant. So uncanny is this gift that she's taken to calling herself the Goddess of Distraction. "Darling," she says when I tell her I'm trying to focus on an enormous project, "Let me take you away from all this!"

There's something about the state of being unable (or unwilling) to focus that draws more unfocused energy magnetically toward you. Like attracts like; distraction invites more distraction. If Sybil doesn't call me at times like this, it's a safe bet someone else will. Or I'll start having some minor but intractable problem with the computer. Or (if I'm working at home) one of the cats will toss a hairball. To be perfectly honest, all *three* of these things have happened since I sat down to write this chapter.

If you've ever attempted to meditate, you know this phenomenon as "monkey mind," the state where your consciousness leaps about wildly and refuses to settle in one place. This psychic scattering is a form of resistance to the task at hand, and like all resistance, it's trying to tell you something. But here's the catch: If you stop to figure out what it's trying to tell you, you won't get your work done. Sometimes, especially if you're working under a deadline, you simply have to force yourself to focus in the moment and examine your resistance later.

Okay, fine. But how?

Cultivating the ability to focus at work, as in meditation, is something you achieve over time, by practicing. And as in meditation, the first step is to watch yourself being unfocused, without judging yourself. If this sounds counterproductive, let me point out that watching yourself being unfocused is itself an exercise in focusing.

As you observe yourself being unfocused, you get to know your personal repertoire of distractions—your favorite physical, mental, and emotional stratagems for withdrawing your attention from the task before you. Right now, for example, there's a load of laundry calling to me to take it from the dryer and fold it. I'm pretty sure my chair could be higher, or possibly lower. The cats, both contentedly asleep, could probably use a dab of hairball remedy. And it's been at least five minutes since I checked my e-mail.

Let's see . . . what else? There's a crick in my neck and a twinge in my right sacroiliac joint; I haven't been doing enough yoga lately. There's also a dull ache in my heart for an important friendship that's ending, petering out really, after many years. Then there's a tightness in my throat—an ongoing anxiety about a health problem of my husband's which is probably minor but for which he is undergoing invasive tests. Oh, and I'm carrying around an old grief which has been acting up lately. I'm going to stop the catalogue here. I happen to be the sort of person who leads with her emotions, so I tend to be hyperaware of emotional wounds, old and new, the way athletes are aware of sports injuries. None of these wounds is disabling me right now, but I'm perfectly willing to be distracted by any or all of them.

My point is that this is a *good* day: I'm reasonably well rested, there are no major crises in my life, and the only thing I really have to do is the task in front of me. Yet I'm seething with distractions, because I'm resisting my task, and because being scattered is a normal state for human beings. The distractions themselves are actually quite useful. Observing them wakes you up.

Have you ever gotten angry at someone and then gotten so absorbed in something else you forgot all about your anger? Have you ever, then, caught yourself in the act of reminding yourself to get angry again? ("What was that thing I was so furious about? Oh *yeah*—so and so said such and such. *Boy* am I pissed off!) This act of reminding yourself, like the act of feeling around with your tongue for a canker sore, is a conscious choice: You're choosing to focus on a distraction, but you can just as easily choose to focus on something else. So (here's the point; get ready) the moment you observe yourself being distracted by something, you can choose to bring your attention back to wherever you want it to be. Distraction becomes the path to a focused mind: You learn to focus by pulling your attention back from a state of unfocused-ness time and again.

Distraction can be useful in at least one other way: Applied creatively, it can stop your thought processes from whirring around and around in the same old loops. The trick is to pick the right distraction for the situation at hand. Sometimes, for example, I'll get stuck in some aspect of the writing process and find myself typing and deleting the same sentence over and over, or staring at the same paragraph until I don't see it anymore. That's when I might decide to distract myself by making a cup of tea. This allows me to get up from my desk and walk to the kitchen, thinking of nothing at all except the hot water, the tea, the cup, and (maybe) the cookie. My subconscious mind, meanwhile, continues to work on the writing problem, and a solution often pops into my head before the kettle boils. This (and the cookie) is why the tea distraction is a favorite of mine. If I choose another, less mindless form of distraction—say, calling my friend Sybil—I'm likely to lose my train of thought for good. I don't call Sybil unless I want a good, clean break from whatever work I'm doing.

Which brings me to another point: Goddesses of Distraction like Sybil are supremely useful for helping you take your mind off the things you love to hate about your job. I'm talking about the things you can't change right now, the things you'll stew about if you don't distract yourself creatively. If, for example, the company you work for finds yet another way to make you feel unappreciated, or if your boss falls into his most annoying managerial habit and you just have to live with it, that's the time to invoke your personal Goddess of Distraction. My friend Jennie goes shoe shopping; sometimes, rarely, she actually gets fed up enough to skip out for an entire afternoon and go to a movie. As for me, I call Sybil—not to bitch about work, but to bitch about something completely extraneous, like, say, why nobody pronounces the first "r" in February anymore. Taking a Goddess of Distraction break can stop you from falling into despair about your job by reminding you that you have a life *outside* your job.

Is that (I hear you ask) all there is? Can't we ever learn to become undistractable? No, and furthermore, we wouldn't want to. Wrestling with distraction is an important aspect of spiritual practice. What we hunger for at work (and at play, and in prayer) is the famous "flow" state, that feeling of utter absorption, of connection to a greater reality—the feeling shared by artists and mystics. Being human, we can't always be in that flow state, but we can find our way to it more often by becoming awake to our own distractions, by getting to know them and use them creatively.

However, we don't automatically achieve flow by learning to focus. Sometimes we achieve something else entirely: We focus on our work only to find we basically don't like the work. We've been distracting ourselves, in turns out, because we really don't want to be doing this task at all.

What if this happens to you? What if you start paying attention and become aware of umpteen things you hate about your job? Well, it's better to be awake than asleep: It's better to be aware of a problem than to move through your days in a scattered, distracted, vaguely discontented state. You can address a problem you know about; you can't do anything about one you refuse to be aware of. Besides, most problems turn out to be eminently addressable once you really look at them. It's denying them that gets you into trouble.

Even when we love our work, flow states are gifts. We can prepare ourselves for them, but we can't will them to happen. I once knew an opera singer who had an extraordinary gift for focus. If she was singing a duet with someone who forgot the words or music or otherwise got lost, she never let it rattle her; she always had the presence of mind, and the stage presence, to pull them both through it. She never lorded this gift over her colleagues; she knew it was the sum of experience and temperament and something more, a kind of grace.

When we encounter someone with this kind of focused serenity, we have the sense that they're fulfilling the task they were born to fulfill. I don't know whether you believe you have a larger task to fulfill in life. I think I do, but that's not saying

I'm fully aware of what that task is. Sometimes I think it's made up of an infinite number of smaller tasks, on which I focus fitfully, intermittently, and, very occasionally, brilliantly. Someday when I look back at my life, perhaps I'll know what my larger task was. But for now, it's enough to learn what I can from facing the distractions of the moment.

....

Exercise: Creative Distractedness

Next time you're unable to focus on a task ... wait a minute. Now that I think about it, it's already something of an achievement to realize you're unable to focus. We all put lots of energy into stalling and otherwise avoiding work (see chapter 2), so distraction is second nature to us.

So the *real* first step in this exercise is to ask yourself to notice when you're distracted. Ask yourself something simplistic like, "What task am I supposed to be doing right now? Am I present for it? If not, where am I?"

Take a few moments to evaluate the quality of your presence, or lack thereof, in relation to the work you're doing. Are you (for example) fidgeting? If so, what kind of fidgeting is it? Are you uncomfortable in a specific physical way? Or are you zoning out mentally—trying to concentrate and failing miserably? Without attempting to do anything about it just yet, observe the nature of your distractedness. Make a mental note of what you're feeling, and be specific: "I'm falling asleep." Or "My neck hurts." Or "I have an anxious feeling somewhere in the middle of my chest." (If you find you can't be specific because you're feeling generally unhappy about your job, you may be dancing around the Slough of Suckiness; see chapter 5.)

Now look a bit more closely at the distraction. Is it something you can fix relatively easily? If, for example, you have a crick in your neck, is it worth your while to take a few minutes to make it feel better? Do you need to roll your head around on your neck, bend over and let it hang down, take an aspirin?

Is the distraction something you can't fix here and now? If, for example, you've had a fight with your mate and you're still brooding about it, you need to make a decision to either put off your brooding to a more suitable time, or delve more deeply into what's upsetting you. Bear in mind that there's a task in front of you and that your brooding may have to wait.

Once you've looked at your distraction and dealt with it, either by fixing it here and now or by electing to shelve it until you *can* fix it, bring your attention back to the task, and try once more to focus on it. See if you can go ahead and just plow through it. If your attention wanders again, bring it gently back to the task. Do this as many times as it takes. It's amazing how much work you can get done by simply bringing your attention back every time it wanders. (This book would never have been finished if that weren't true.)

Once you get to know your personal repertoire of distractions, you can start to use them creatively. If you feel fidgety, for instance, you can let yourself fidget for a few minutes, maybe get up, and walk around the office or even around the block, turning that fidgetiness into a mini break that gets your energy moving again. If you can't stop brooding about that fight with your mate no matter how hard you try, maybe that's the thing you really need to be dealing with right now. Don't, in other words, berate yourself for being distracted. Just work with whatever's right in front of you. The most mundane task, or the most trivial distraction, can become a kind of meditation when you approach it mindfully. If you can't focus because you're all over the place, you can at least *be* all over the place.

Mantra for the Bad Days:

When the Goddess of Distraction calls, sometimes
I've just got to pick up the phone.

Chapter 15

Perfectionists Anonymous

A long time ago, though not as long ago as I'd like, I used to write fashion copy. I'd be handed a layout in Greek type—dummy copy indicating how much space I had to fill—and I'd sit staring at the pictures on the page, trying to think up words to describe them. Writing fashion copy can be fun if you can forget you're creating something disposable. You're limited to the number of lines and characters the art director sees fit to give you—so not only do you have to come up with the right words, they have to be the right length. And since every descriptive phrase you come up with, if it's any good, has already been thought of a thousand thousand times before, it's a challenge to do anything fresh. I remember doing a lot more sitting and staring than writing, and producing quite a lot of bad copy before coming up with something not so bad.

Once, I had to write the text for a page about very small

evening bags—purses so tiny you couldn't get a comb into them, let alone a wallet. They were silly but fun, and I spent at least half an hour trying to write a headline describing them. Everything I came up with was awful: "Little Baby Baggies." "Palm This!" "A Fistful of Sequins." "Itty Bitty Teeny Tiny Totes." Finally, the right title popped into my head, seemingly unbidden: "Sleight-of-Hand Bags." It even worked with the picture. My editor thought it was very clever, but then, she didn't see the dozens of rejects.

My point—there actually is a relevant point here—is that I was a good copy writer because I let myself be relaxed about being a *bad* copy writer. I knew that you often have to spew out endless drivel to come up with one or two lines of gold, and that, in the words of one of the rockers in *This Is Spinal Tap,* there's a very fine line between clever and stupid. Being unafraid to write stupid copy helped me get loose enough to write clever stuff once in a while.

I never went to school to learn to write fashion copy. I just sat down and did it because it seemed a decent way to pay the rent, which I very much needed to pay. I did, however, go to school to learn how to sing, and *boy* was I not relaxed about being a bad singer. If a note came out of my mouth that wasn't perfect, if I couldn't master a tricky run on the first or second try, if my listeners weren't prostrate with adulation (they usually weren't), then I was a failure. My parents were wasting their tuition money, and I was wasting my life. Even though I knew that singing is, as one of my teachers used to say, a very big art, and that it takes time to develop a voice, I panicked whenever I sang something imperfectly. I couldn't forgive myself for not being a better singer than I was.

In fact, I wasn't getting very good teaching at the conservatory. Nobody there showed me the basics of good singing—there are a shocking number of singing teachers who don't know them and can't teach them—so I never improved much. Years later, after I finally found a teacher who knew what he was doing, I realized how badly I'd been shortchanged. But I couldn't have understood this while I was in school, because back then I identified too deeply with the idea of being a singer. If I wasn't a singer, I was nobody. If I didn't improve, it meant my voice just wasn't good enough, which meant that *I* wasn't good enough.

Looking back on all this, I can see the benefit of having regarded myself as a failed musician for so many years: It allowed me to become a successful magazine professional. All the drama, all the emotional freight of "failing," was conveniently stored in the part of my psyche that was devoted to music—leaving the rest of me free to go about the business of learning a craft and building a career. The singer had to be perfect, but the writer was free to be imperfect. The writer, I might add, was a lot happier than the singer.

Having been both a perfectionist and an imperfectionist (if there is such a word), I can tell you that perfectionism absolutely paralyzes you. Any task that has to be done perfectly becomes a task that can make or break you. Because your whole identity is somehow riding on it, you can't let yourself screw up. So you take no pleasure in the task and derive no satisfaction from the result, which can't possibly be good enough.

A task that can be done *im*perfectly, by contrast, is a task you can have fun with—a task you can throw all your creativity at just to see what sticks. Because you're still learning how to master it (as we're all still learning everything we do, even the stuff we're good at), you can watch yourself falling down and picking yourself up and have the luxury of trying to figure out where you went wrong. Not to mention the endless fun of looking at your mistakes.

Granted, there are some tasks that leave little room for failure. I wouldn't want to be on the receiving end of a brain surgeon's mistake, and I expect a great chef to serve me a great soufflé, especially if he's charging me a lot for it. For that matter, I'm not going to show you any rough drafts of my writing. It *is* important to cultivate a certain level of professionalism. But you can't cultivate it unless you let yourself relax into your work. You can sense the relaxation in the hand of a master. You can see it in Picasso's line, hear it in Bach's counterpoint, or in Shakespeare's poetry. Of course, these men were geniuses, but they were also driven to practice their craft obsessively—to experiment fearlessly—until it took them farther than anyone could have imagined.

Think about Olympic figure skaters. All of them practice and practice their triple and quadruple jumps until they can do them flawlessly; all have strong techniques to fall back on. But when they're competing for medals with the world watching, when they know they have to be perfect, they often miss jumps they've aced in practice. The skaters who win are the ones who not only have technique and experience, but who can also connect in the moment with their love of skating and relax into their joy in doing what they do.

Take a few moments to think about the tasks you usually feel relaxed about, at work and at home, and the tasks that make you tense up just thinking about them. Ask yourself: In what areas of my life do I expect myself to be perfect, and how does that perfectionism make me feel? And: Does the thought of being paid to do a task make me more nervous about getting it right?

My friend Liz, an extremely capable executive, knows that her employers highly value her work. They keep giving her raises and telling her how great she is, among other things. But she still has a hard time believing she's not going to be fired any minute. Even though she's already chalked up many successes in her current job, even though she has years of experience to draw on, she feels paralyzed whenever she has to embark on a new project. Every new task feels like an all-or-nothing proposition: Either she'll do it brilliantly or she'll fail miserably. "You would never know it to look at me," she says, "But inside, I'm a ball of fear."

I happen to know that Liz is accustomed to being a ball of fear. She grew up in a family that presented a "perfect" appearance to the world: They lived in a beautiful house in an upscale neighborhood, attended the best schools, wore expensive clothes, went to the right church, gave to the right charities. Presentation was everything. It helped gloss over certain untidy realities, such as the alcoholism of one of Liz's parents and the juvenile record of one of her siblings. Liz's childhood landscape was planted with emotional landmines, but you would never have known it to look at her.

For as long as she can remember, Liz has presented a veneer of quiet confidence while being inwardly terrified she'll slip up and reveal how screamingly imperfect she is. By this time, she has lived a certain number of decades and never once achieved perfection. But she has, as I said, achieved some real successes, both personally and professionally. She has sustained loving human relationships, been a good wife and mother, and a breadwinner. So she's not quite the ball of fear she once was. In fact, she's learned that her perfectionism, far from ensuring better results in her endeavors, buys her nothing but fear and anxiety. Still, she falls into her old habit of perfectionism whenever she faces any new project, even though she knows better.

Why should anyone, even someone as accomplished as Liz, still cling to perfectionism? The short answer is that when a person first adopts perfectionism, it represents a security blanket—a way out of difficulty, a ray of hope. In Liz's childhood, she never knew whether she would be coming home to a loving, sober mother or an irrational, drunk mother. She had no control at all over her environment, but she *did* have some control over her own actions. "If I can be very, very good all the time," she told herself, "nobody will have any reason to get mad at me." It didn't work, of course, but it gave her something to cling to.

Most of us, I venture to say, have some version of this conversation with ourselves as children. The world is a scary, unpredictable place, and the only thing we can actually control to some degree is our own behavior. So we get into the habit of bullying ourselves to be better than we actually are. Or we attempt to shield ourselves from punishment by punishing ourselves before anyone else can. It's a strategy that pretty much guarantees we'll suffer, but hey—better the devil you know than the devil you don't, right? Liz has become so accustomed to being a ball of fear when she starts something new that she unconsciously regards her fear as a kind of good-luck charm: First she experiences the terror, and then she succeeds at whatever she's trying. What she doesn't quite realize yet is that she doesn't need the terror anymore. She can proceed directly to the success if she wants to.

Perfectionism is always Old Stuff—a habit we've adopted so long ago we're barely aware it's kicking in. So what can we do about it? Well, for one thing, if we're so inclined, we can try to sort out the reasons we adopted a perfectionist approach in the first place—revisit our ancient childhood feelings, figure out why we once told ourselves we had to be perfect, and ask ourselves whether we really need to be so hard on ourselves anymore. This, of course, is a psychological knot that can take years to unravel. What are we supposed to do with our perfectionist urges in the meantime? What do we do if fear grips us as we're facing a deadline, or sitting among our peers in a conference room, or standing before our boss?

The only thing we really *can* do is to note our own panic, then simply plunge into the work at hand. We can learn to recognize the signs of our own brand of perfectionism: the tightening in the throat, the flutter in the gut, the grim joylessness that tells us we're approaching a task as though it were a measure of our self-worth. We can acknowledge our own fear without succumbing to it.

As my friend Liz says, "By this time, I know that the only way to get through my fear of doing something new is to pray I'll be carried through my task, and then to *just go ahead and do it.*"

She's right. Dealing with perfectionism in the moment calls for a leap of faith—faith that you won't bomb completely, faith that your whole world won't crash if you do fail, faith that you'll be All Right, even if you're not perfect.

Look at it this way: If you do bomb (and everybody bombs once in a while), you're going to have to deal with the repercussions no matter what. Beating up on yourself won't help the situation; it will only make you more miserable. So you may as well let go of your perfectionism, see what happens, and try to enjoy the ride.

....

Exercise: Request Permission to Screw Up, Sir

Think of a task you're usually a perfectionist about—something you get mad at yourself for screwing up. This can be any endeavor in which you tense up for fear of making a mistake, whether it's speaking in public, coming up with ideas in a meeting, writing a memo, rolling out pastry, or serving a tennis ball.

Envision yourself approaching this task. Specifically, envision the moment when fear or anxiety grips you, the moment when you tell yourself some version of, "I *have* to get this right!" or "I'm going to blow this, I just know it!" Live in this imagined moment for a while. As you feel your breath and body tightening up, say to yourself: "This is what my brand of perfectionism feels like. Is it really doing me any earthly good?"

The purpose of this exercise is not so much to figure out *why* you're a perfectionist about this particular endeavor, though you can certainly try to do so if you like. The real point is to observe the tension your perfectionism creates in you. How can you possibly give your best to a task when you've twisted yourself into a ball of fear?

Once you've experienced this tension for a while, imagine saying to yourself, "Okay, you're off the hook. I give you permission to mess this up. You don't *have* to mess up, mind you, but if it happens, it happens, and it won't be the end of the world."

I'm asking you to practice giving yourself permission to be imperfect, and to do it whenever you come up against your own perfectionism. You're the only person who can let yourself off this particular hook. So stop demanding that you live up to some unrealistic standard and just do the damn task, whatever it is. If you find it hard to stop beating up on yourself, well, don't expect yourself to be perfect at letting go of your perfectionism, either.

For extra credit, give yourself permission to mess up gloriously once in a while. Share a really stupid idea in a meeting and see whether it sparks somebody else to come up with a better one. Attempt an activity you have absolutely no natural aptitude for and see if you can have fun doing it badly. Try to make some mistakes you can laugh at. You'll have a better time, and a better track record, in the long run.

. . . .

One more thing: Perfectionism is contagious. If you tend to beat up on yourself, you may tend to beat up on your staff, too, if you have a staff. If your boss is a perfectionist, you may allow his or her perfectionism to trigger yours. The only way to stop this from

happening is to honor yourself as the imperfect being you are—
and to let yourself off the hook as often as you have to.

> **Mantra for the Bad Days:**
> Anything worth doing is worth screwing up royally.

Chapter 16   "It's Business."

KEYWORD

compassion

After four years as an assistant manager at the Over Your Head Corp., a manufacturer of roofing materials, George is being laid off. His boss, Jules, who is genuinely sorry to see him go, assures him that his performance has been sterling in every way, and that if it were up to him, George would keep his job. But housing starts are down and profits are off—through no fault of George's—and the company has to become leaner and meaner. So George's department is being downsized, and George, having the least seniority, has to go. "We're really sorry to lose you," Jules tells him, not quite looking him in the eye. "But you understand . . . it's business."

Andy runs a small independent printing firm, which is under contract to several financial services companies. When the time comes to renew his contract with his biggest client, MoJo & Partners, Andy calls Edna, his contact at MoJo, to discuss the terms. Edna is cordial but evasive. She tells Andy his terms sound reasonable, and that she'll talk to her management and get back to him. She never does get back to him, though, and when Andy finally reaches her two weeks later, Edna tells him regretfully that MoJo has decided to give its business to another printer. "I'm sorry I couldn't be more direct with you," she says, "but the decision was out of my hands. The partners wanted to go with a larger firm that could give them deeper discounts. I've really enjoyed working with you, but you understand . . . it's business."

"It's business." I'm sure you've heard these words as often as I have, and perhaps even said them yourself. In my experience, they're usually spoken in defense of behavior that protects a company's bottom line at the expense of individual human beings. Jules speaks them to George to signify that he really is on George's side, but that his personal loyalty is a candle in the wind of corporate necessity, as it were. Edna speaks them to Andy to signify that she knows it was crummy of her to blindside him, but that she is an employee of MoJo and must represent MoJo's interests even if it means trampling his.

Both Jules and Edna are right, in a sense. Even if the Over Your Head Corp. has gotten itself into financial hot water through sheer managerial stupidity, the water really is hot and the layoffs really are necessary, probably. And even if MoJo & Partners has chosen to dump Andy's firm without giving Andy a chance to compete for its business, the firm is perfectly within its rights to do so. So why can't Jules look George in the eye? And why does Edna feel a stab of guilt whenever she remembers her valedictory conversation with Andy? Because they both had to harden their hearts in order to carry out the business directives they'd been given, and it didn't feel good.

Many of us believe, consciously or not, that earning a living requires a hardening of the heart at some point. Business is, after all, a numbers game, seemingly a zero-sum game: you either make a profit or post a loss; you either win or lose; and if you lose, someone else wins. Human compassion can seem like a reckless soft-heartedness. If you retain staff instead of laying people off during a recession, for example, your bloated payroll costs may endanger your entire enterprise. There's a reason why the word "lean" is usually paired with the word "mean" in business parlance.

I have a music degree, not an MBA, so I'm not going to try to pretend I'm an expert in the science of profit and loss, or that I'm particularly competitive by temperament. I do know, however, that if you work for a successful company—one that has a bigger market share and a higher profit margin than its competition—you'll probably enjoy more prestige, more job security, and possibly a higher salary than if you work for a less successful firm. If your company keeps a heartless eye on the bottom line, in other words, you benefit.

Furthermore, if you work within any kind of hierarchy, you probably aren't given much of a choice about carrying out corporate directives. Jules had his marching orders to let George go, and Edna had no say in choosing which vendors her firm would hire. But they both felt lousy about their actions anyway. Even if there are solid business reasons for doing something that hurts a fellow human being, even if you have no choice *but* to do it, it still feels awful. That's why we grit our teeth and tell ourselves, "It's business." What we're really saying is, "There's no place for personal feelings here." Or even: "I don't *want* to feel this. It's too painful." If we say these things to ourselves often enough, we run the risk of deadening our capacity to feel.

I've chosen to focus on the words "It's business" because to me, they capture that heart-hardening moment so perfectly. Jules feels guilty when he thinks about George's wife and kids, who will sorely feel the loss of his income. He knows he can't offer any real support outside of a good job reference, so he also feels helpless. And he's nervous about his own job security.

It seems to him that George is losing his job so Jules can keep his—that zero-sum game again. In other words, he's afraid—of losing his job, his livelihood, his sense of self-worth. And when fear creeps in, compassion becomes a luxury. He has no choice but to harden his heart. This, to him, is business.

Edna, too, is afraid. She's pretty low on the totem pole at MoJo & Partners. She privately believes her bosses are ruthless bastards, and she has a lot of sympathy for small vendors like Andy. When her bosses told her to dump him and hire someone else she felt so bad she didn't know how to handle it. So she dodged his calls and broke the news to him at the last possible minute, feeling like an absolute rat. Could she have managed the situation more diplomatically? Probably, but the outcome would still have been the same: Andy losing his biggest client. Edna feels powerless. She needs her job. She and Andy are little guys, and in business, little guys get the short end of the stick.

The truth is that we're all little guys. Whether we're at the top or the bottom of the totem pole, we're all human beings with human bodies and psyches. We need food, shelter, and a sense of security and self-worth. Andy, Edna, and Edna's bosses all have mortgages and mouths to feed. They may seem to have different sets of worries, but they really all have the same worry:

"IT'S BUSINESS."

Will I survive? Will my family survive? Can I take care of myself and those I love? So when they steel themselves and say, "It's business," they're actually talking about something deeply personal. Raw survival is about as personal as you can get.

So here's my question: Is it possible to take care of business—to do what you have to do to survive—without hardening your heart to the suffering of others? Is it possible to tend to the bottom line and still keep your soul intact, or at least not hate yourself at the end of the day? Can you be competitive *and* compassionate? Is business—is life—really a zero-sum game?

I suppose you're expecting a straight answer from me, and I wish I had one. I want to tell you that life is *not* a zero-sum game; that it really *is* possible to run a business in such a way that everybody wins at least part of the time; that of *course* we can all find compassion within ourselves if we're willing to look for it. I actually believe these things. But I also know that our lives and jobs are imperfect. In real life, it is not possible to avoid suffering—our own, or that of others. Like Jules and Edna, we are thrown into situations that challenge our humanity and compassion. We find ourselves swimming in shark-infested waters. We are confronted with our own fears of not measuring up, of failing, of being helpless. We get scared, we harden our hearts, we treat others badly, we feel lousy about it, we cut off our feelings. We want to think of ourselves as compassionate beings, but in reality, our compassion comes and goes.

What can we do about this? We can't force ourselves to be compassionate. But we can observe, *without judging ourselves,* our own failures of compassion. We can let ourselves feel the fear that may be causing us to harden our hearts. We can ask ourselves whether there isn't some way to keep our hearts open and still take care of business. We can look, in other words, at the imperfection in front of us, taking it on faith that imperfection is one of our greatest teachers.

Exercise: Welcoming the Pang of Compassion

Has there ever been a time when you've felt you had to harden your heart at work? When you've had to draw a line between your feelings for another human being and the realities of business? Have you ever felt compelled by business interests to treat someone in a way that made you feel guilty? Try to think of one such time. Don't judge yourself; the point of this exercise is to learn something useful, not to pile on still more guilt.

I can remember, for example, when one of my colleagues experienced a personal meltdown that rendered her unable to carry her share of the workload. Granted, she was going through a very tough time—a rocky marriage, trouble with a stepchild, hormonal fluctuations that left her foggy and unfocused. But I felt my compassion fail when I had to take over some of her work while she negotiated her various crises. "This staff is too small to pick up her slack," I found myself thinking. "She has to go. We're the herd; she's the wounded antelope. It's business." My own ruthlessness made me very uncomfortable.

If the staff had been bigger, we could have carried her for a while, but our company (we felt) squeezed us to the limit. The staff was so lean we *had* to be mean. (Think about it: The money a company is willing to spend on its staff has a major effect on morale.) So I was angry at my own management, and worried about my ability to get the extra work done. When I said, "It's business," I was really saying, "This place doesn't value its employees, so I can't have the luxury of valuing my foundering colleague." I was also saying, "This place doesn't value *me*. Nobody here cares whether *I* burn out." In other words, I felt unvalued and unsupported, and that scared me. Beneath my lack of compassion lay an old, existential fear of being alone and helpless.

Whenever you feel yourself hardening your heart toward someone at work, you can be pretty sure that something is touching off a deep, unspoken fear in you. It may be that your workplace culture is the catalyst for this fear. Edna, for example, worked in a culture of ruthless people; she felt she had to adopt **175**

their ruthlessness to hold on to her job. George worked in a company where management was running scared, and some of that fear was passed along to him.

Okay. Think again about that time you hardened your heart at work. Was there anything in your workplace culture that made you feel it was necessary to be a little bit ruthless? I'm not saying your culture is totally at fault here; I'm just saying that the culture can have an enormous effect on your feelings and actions, and it's useful to know what that effect is.

Now ask yourself: *Was there anything about this situation that made me feel afraid? Was there something that seemed to threaten my own safety or security?* Don't try to force an answer; just put the question to yourself and see what comes to you. As I said, we all live with our own little-guy fears of not being good enough, or of not being able to provide for ourselves and our families, and those fears are usually not too far from the surface.

If we learn to observe our fear, we learn that fear is a transient thing. It comes in waves, and then it goes. If we let ourselves feel our fear—which, after all, we've felt many times before—we can say, "Ah, there's the fear again." Then we can let it go, at least for the moment; or we can live with it, knowing it will leave us eventually. Believe it or not, feeling our own fear allows us to be more compassionate toward others, because we can be sensitive to their fear as well. It may not change our actions, but it helps us keep our hearts open.

We all experience failures in compassion. Don't be discouraged by yours; simply observe them. Even if all you can say is, "I wish I could have more compassion for this person," you're opening the door to feeling more compassion. You may not be able to change the business reality; you may still have to act in a way that makes you uncomfortable. But at least you can bring your whole self to the situation, fear, ambivalence, ruthlessness, and all.

· ·

When a job situation forces you to harden your heart, you feel a little pang—the pang of your moral compass kicking in. That pang is a signal that you're feeling threatened by something, threatened enough to want to cut off your own feelings. I'm asking you to welcome that pang, and the tangled feelings it brings with it. It will help you see yourself, and your colleagues, more clearly in the present moment. And it will help you see your own fear for what it is: a presence in your life, but not your master.

Mantra for the Bad Days:
When I can't feel compassion for someone else, that's when I need to have some for myself.

Chapter 17

Love Thy Colleague

KEYWORD

love

If you've stayed with me until this point, you've probably picked up on a fundamental flaw of self-help books like this one: I've been writing as though being a spiritual person were your only care in the world—as though you were free to devote most of your energy to bringing your best self to your job. But of course you're not. Real life isn't like that.

In real life—assuming your life is anything like mine—there are loose ends all over the place. Huge, hairy stresses compete for your attention. You don't live in a monastic cell furnished chastely yet chicly with a meditation cushion and an artistic scattering of Japanese river rocks. You live in a house, or an apartment, *with other people who need you*. If these other people don't actually live with you, they're at the other end of your telephone. In any case, you couldn't escape them even if you wanted to; they are your community.

In real life, you are seeking or sustaining a love relationship—a marriage, perhaps. This, as we know, is a life's work in itself, but it demands exponentially more of you if you also have children. Especially small children. Or, God help you, adolescent children. Being there for your nearest and dearest—being a lover, a parent, a referee, a true friend—is a full-time job, and it isn't even your day job. It's your day-and-night job. Your family's joys are your joys, and their problems are your problems.

Which reminds me: In real life, you may have parents who are getting to an age or state of infirmity where they need you to help take care of them—whether or not you have the time, inclination, or psychic strength for the task.

In real life, you have friendships that matter to you, friendships that need your attention in order to thrive. You have neighbors to watch over, or at least be civil to. You may have family obligations: parent-teacher conferences, soccer games, complicated carpooling arrangements. You definitely have a physical body that needs to be fed, rested, and exercised so it won't crash on you, bringing the entire edifice of your life down with it. Oh, and there's that other little thing, your day job.

In other words, you have a life that's already crowded with obligations, some welcome, some not. How can your personal spiritual growth be anywhere near the top of your priority list? And how can your job—your earthbound, paycheck-generating job—possibly become an active source of spiritual sustenance?

By this time, you know me well enough to know I believe spirituality is not a separate area of your life; it embraces the whole of your life. Your spirituality lies in the present moment—in the task that's right in front of you, whether that task is family related or work related. If you want your job to be a source of spiritual sustenance, all you really need to do is to start treating it as if it already were one. All you need to do, in other words, is to bring your whole self to your job, including the part of you that loves.

I'm not being sappy here. I'm being extremely practical. It's love, after all, that connects us with others and with our own deepest selves. We work hard at maintaining our loving relationships because we know that love takes work, and we're willing to do that work to keep love flowing in our lives. So why not keep it flowing in *all* areas of our lives? Why not at least remind ourselves, at every possible minute, of our own capacity to love—our potential for love—in the context of our real lives?

The people you work with are not necessarily people you wish to be close to. You may not even particularly like them, and I'm certainly not saying you *have* to like them. I am, however, asking you to consider loving them—or at least behaving as though they were worthy of love. They'll benefit from this, and so will you, in ways that may surprise you.

I've mentioned my friend Joan, who has two children and works full time as a pathologist in a local hospital. Joan is on call (meaning she can't schedule any other activities) two nights a week and every third weekend. Her husband was laid off recently, so while he's not contributing much income at the moment, he is able to do the lion's share of carpooling and homework supervision. Which is a good thing, because Joan's widowed mother has had a series of strokes that have left her increasingly disabled and depressed, and Joan is the de facto caregiver. This means she has to hire and supervise an ever-changing crew of home health aides. It also means she has to be ready to respond to her mother's escalating, often irrational demands for Joan's personal attention.

Joan considers herself a spiritual person, though she doesn't advertise herself as such. She draws a good deal of sustenance from creating a safe, loving home for her husband and daughters, and from being an active member of her synagogue. But the combined demands of her three "careers"—as a physician and breadwinner, as a wife and mother, and as a caregiver—have pushed her past the edge of exhaustion. She doesn't get nearly enough sleep, and she has an unfortunate tendency to

try to bridge the energy gap with chocolate. (I can relate.)
However, Joan does have an unexpected source of spiritual
strength: She makes a conscious effort to give more, rather
than less, of herself to the people she works with.

"When I'm under a lot of stress, I need my colleagues more
than ever," she told me. "For one thing, if I'm tired, I need to
rely on them to confirm a tricky diagnosis. When patients' lives
are at stake, we really can't afford to make mistakes. But I also
find that if we make an effort to be there for each other personally as well as professionally, we create a community of caring
that sustains us through the tough times. So if someone I work
with has a problem at home or at work, I try to help, even if
I'm already overextended. I take the time to listen to my colleagues, and as a result, my colleagues listen to me."

Note that Joan talks about *creating* a community of caring.
As I'm sure you know, it's not a given that people who work
together will come to care about each other. Joan has worked
in groups where a more competitive spirit prevailed, where it
was much harder to create an environment of mutual support.
But even in those situations, Joan's policy has been to create
friendships wherever she can, and to be as caring as she can.
Being a good, ethical person is a central spiritual value for her.
She knows from experience that giving is the same thing as
receiving, and that being a giving person will actually sustain

her when her life becomes overwhelming. (Giving *is* the same thing as receiving, and the only way to know it is through experience.)

If all this sounds too touchy-feely for you, I understand. Love may be the last thing you want to think about in your particular workplace. You may not *want* to create a community of caring at work, especially if you have a perfectly good one at home. I happen to believe you need all the caring you can get (or give) in life, but sometimes you just have to put business first and caring second. Right?

Well, no. Caring *is* good business, on both a personal level and a corporate level. If you've been in the working world a while, you know there are people in every industry who have great reputations as bosses: They're fair and supportive, they have high standards, and they bring out the best in their staffs. Other bosses have well-deserved reputations for being monsters: They're abusive, aggressive, and ego-driven. I've worked for both types, and I can tell you that either type can run a profit-making enterprise. But ego-driven bosses have a harder time keeping good people; their shops are more chaotic, less efficient. Ego-driven bosses often refuse to see their subordinates' potential, so a lot of that potential goes untapped. Caring bosses, on the other hand, respect their subordinates, and are often rewarded with the kind of performance and loyalty money can't buy.

It's no longer a business truism that nice guys finish last. Internet executive Tim Sanders, in his book *Love Is the Killer App: How to Win Business and Influence Friends,* argues that being generous—with your contacts, your experience, and your humanity—is the key to success. "The less you expect for acts of professional generosity," writes Sanders, "the more you will receive."

I believe Sanders is right, and I think his advice holds true whether you're running your own company or just punching a clock. If you are generous with your compassion, your respect, and, yes, your love, you'll profit in some way. Obviously, it never hurts to do a favor for a colleague or business acquaintance—to offer your time, your Rolodex, or your listening ear to someone who needs a friend. My point is that the more you give of yourself to others, the more your job will feel like part of your spiritual path, regardless of whether your favors are ever returned.

Okay, but what if you work with someone you actively dislike? Or with someone who will take advantage of your generosity if you're dumb enough to offer it?

Mark and Dave are computer network specialists for a midsize manufacturing firm. Dave has personal problems—marital difficulties, health issues, low-level depression—that result in his missing a lot of work, and Mark has to pick up the slack. Their supervisor understands the situation but says that Mark will just have to do the best he can until Dave finds a way to deal with his difficulties. So Mark muddles through, staggering under the workload, and resenting every minute of it. He thinks Dave is whiny, self-pitying, and way too good at finding excuses for slacking off.

Mark doesn't want to hear about Dave's personal problems, which Dave is happy to discuss for hours on end. He just wants to do his job, and he wishes Dave would do *his*. One day, though, Mark has a sudden flash of compassion. He's installing a new software package when he thinks to himself, "Dave would probably enjoy working with this program. It's really too bad the guy has so many problems. I like to think I'd handle them differently if I were him, but hey—I'm *not* him. I'm luckier than he is."

Suddenly Mark feels grateful for his own good fortune: his health, his marriage, his pleasure in his work. In that moment, he's able to let go of his habitual judgment of Dave—that he's lazy and self-dramatizing—and see him as a fellow human being struggling to create a good life for himself. Then something unexpected happens: Mark feels a flash of respect for Dave's struggle. And along with that respect, he feels—of all things—love. Not enormous love, mind you; just enough to make him see Dave as somebody who might conceivably be lovable. He's never seen him as remotely lovable before.

Mark and Dave will probably never be pals, but palhood is not the point. Love is the point. If Mark can learn to remind himself of that brief moment when he felt compassion and even love for Dave, he may come to feel differently about his colleague. He'll still have to do more than his share of work, but perhaps he'll no longer feel so angry about it, so personally wronged. He may even begin to treat Dave a little more gently, and Dave will sense it. When someone cares about you, you know it, even if nothing much is said.

This is the kind of thing I'm talking about when I suggest you consider loving the people you work with. You don't have to pretend you care about them when you don't, and you certainly don't have to make yourself their personal doormat. But you can, perhaps, cultivate a little empathy, which is a doorway to love. It begins with a click of consciousness, a flash of compassion, a nanosecond's realization that your colleagues, too, are on a spiritual path. All I'm asking you to do is take that nanosecond and prize it.

Exercise: Intending to Love

In the Theravada tradition of Buddhism, there's a meditation called Universal Loving Kindness, which you do first thing in the morning, last thing at night, and at the beginning of each meditation session. Its purpose is to help free you, temporarily, from whatever negative emotion or obsession is distracting you at the moment. It also helps you cultivate the understanding that loving yourself and loving other people are one and the same thing.

You begin this meditation by wishing good things for yourself: *May I be well, happy, and peaceful. May no harm come to me. May no difficulties come to me. May I meet with success. May I also have the patience, courage, understanding, and determination to meet and overcome inevitable difficulties, problems, and failures in life.* (This prayer comes from *Mindfulness in Plain English* by Venerable Henepola Gunaratana, published in 1991 by Wisdom Publications in Boston.) You can phrase it more simply if you like. You might say something like: *May I be well and happy; may I be free from pain and fear; may I know how worthy of love I am.* The idea is to wish yourself well and mean it.

Then you extend these good wishes to the other people in your life, starting with your nearest and dearest: *May my husband [wife] be well and happy; may [s]he be free from pain and fear; may [s]he know how worthy of love [s]he is.* Then you direct the same positive thoughts to your children, your parents, your siblings, your close friends, in whatever order feels right to you.

Then comes the interesting part: You extend the same good wishes to people outside your customary circle of caring—to your colleagues, to your enemies (yes, your enemies), to total strangers, and to all living beings. The purpose of this meditation is not to actually *feel* lovingkindness toward everyone on earth— this isn't something you can will yourself to do, after all—but to *intend* to feel it, to open yourself to the possibility of feeling it. To *imagine* yourself feeling it.

Try doing this meditation just once, to see how it feels: Wish blessings on yourself (don't skip this step!), then on those closest to you, then on the other people in your life, including people you don't like and don't even know. Say the words to yourself, and try to feel an intention to mean them.

Now focus on a specific person you work with, and wish the same blessings on him or her. Try to see that person as someone struggling to live a good life, someone worthy of love. Hold that person in your heart, and wish him or her well. For extra credit, try extending your blessings to a colleague you can't stand. You can go right back to loathing him or her when you're done. But try for just one moment to imagine that you and this person are blessed, and that you're here to enrich each other's lives in some way. Because you are.

Mantra for the Bad Days:

May I know how worthy of love I am. May we all know
how worthy of love we are.

Chapter 18 Lunch

There's an old Zen Buddhist story about a monk who finally achieves enlightenment after years and years of meditation. Someone asks him how he feels in his new enlightened state, and he says, "the same as I felt before."

Well, of course. He's still the same monk, living the same monk's life in the same monk's body. He may have achieved a new level of understanding—of *knowing*—but he's still himself, and he's still here. As the saying goes: "Before enlightenment, chop wood, carry water. After enlightenment, chop wood, carry water." Nowhere is it written that you will no longer get tired, bored, or angry about chopping and carrying once you've moved to a new level of spiritual understanding. But the experience of fatigue, boredom, or anger will have a different quality, a different taste.

To those of us with central heating and indoor plumbing, the "chop wood, carry water" metaphor seems picturesquely remote and Zen-like: *Ah yes—wood is fuel for the fire that sustains us; water is the water of life. We can be grateful to the tree that gives us wood and the spring that gives us water, and feel our oneness with the cycle of life.* Yeah, right, fine, but if we actually had to chop our own wood and carry our own water every day, we would know it for the endless, thankless, back-breaking work it is. Life is hard, even when it's good. Providing food and shelter for ourselves is a constant struggle, even if we're toting takeout sushi home to a condo with a satellite dish. Even a good job is physically and psychically draining. Many of the hours we spend at work are unproductive; many of the tasks we get paid to do are meaningless. Before enlightenment, push paper, attend meetings. After enlightenment, push paper, attend meetings.

Bringing our whole selves to work, spirituality and all, is difficult. And messy. If we attempt to focus single-mindedly on a task, we slam head-on into our own resistance to it. If we try to bring our full attention to our jobs, we inevitably come up against our own authority issues, our foiled hopes and dreams, our anxieties about money—everything that's unfinished, unresolved, and unsatisfactory about our lives.

This is why it's noble, in the Buddhist sense of a "noble" truth, to attempt to be truly present in the moment: The present moment is where we encounter our imperfect selves and our imperfect lives, and are thereby made aware of the spiritual task before us. The present moment is where we get to acknowledge our own nobility for taking on such a task. The present moment is where we get to love life as it is, and to love ourselves as we are.

It's in the grittiness of the present moment that we encounter holiness. It's in the mundaneness and frustration of our day-to-day jobs that we encounter our own divinity. The more we're willing to see ourselves as we are, and our jobs as they are, the more we know how that newly-enlightened monk felt: the same, and different. Human, and holy.

If I had to boil this whole book down to one idea, it would be this: *A spiritual path is not about getting there. It's about being here. You're following your path, but your path is also carrying you. There is no "wrong" way to proceed: Open your eyes, and you'll be where you need to be.*

Which brings me to my final point. Since you're a spiritual being on a spiritual path every minute of your life, you might as well relax. Stop worrying about measuring up to some idealized notion of who you're supposed to be, and trust that you're *already* exactly who you're supposed to be. Try to enjoy the ride.

My friend Sybil, the Goddess of Distraction, called me one morning a few years ago to lament a particularly trying situation at her job. We've both forgotten what it was—one of her bosses being a selfish bitch and making everyone else on the staff suffer, I think. Sybil had examined the problem from every possible angle; she'd felt her anger and frustration, and had the requisite conversation with Human Resources. But she couldn't stop feeling furious at the injustice of it all. She ranted on and on about what an unhappy place her formerly happy office had become. "I've just *had* it!" she said. "What am I supposed to *do* about a situation like this?"

"Well," I said, "Why not think about what you want to have for lunch?"

I heard a swift intake of breath, then silence: the sound of Enlightenment. "You know," she said after a moment, "I think that's the single best piece of advice anyone's ever given me."

Now, I happened to know that Sybil could be profitably distracted by the thought of a sausage calzone from Rico's, but that wasn't the enlightening part. The enlightening part was her realization that at any given moment, she could disconnect from her tangled, angry feelings and focus on something more global and benign. Like lunch. Her problem, whatever it was, would still be there when she turned her attention to it once more. So she didn't have to keep chasing it in the same angry circles all day long. She could have a calzone instead.

And that, good reader, is my parting advice to you: Face the imperfections of the workplace lightly. Acknowledge your frustrations and let them go. Be as kind to yourself as you possibly can, because you're doing something noble and difficult and holy just by living your life and earning your living. Chop wood, carry water. Eat the calzone.

Mantra for the Bad Days:

What do I want for lunch?

Keywords Cheat Sheet

Wait . . . what was that deep, important insight I just had? Spiritual understanding has a maddening tendency to disappear (or seem to disappear) as mysteriously as it appears. Being human, we forget a lot of the stuff we've struggled so hard to learn: Now we get it, now we don't. Fortunately, most major insights come right back to us with a little of the right kind of prodding.

That's what this Cheat Sheet is for. It's a glossary that summarizes, in handy-dandy digest form, the core concepts in this book. When you find yourself feeling angry, unhappy, or frustrated in your job, studying one or more of these "keywords" may help remind you why, and point you toward a solution.

Each listing below is a distillation—a short version—of ideas treated at length in the main body of this book. For a full discussion of each keyword, turn to the relevant chapter, also listed below.

Authority (Chapter 6). The way we relate to our bosses—and our underlings—is a direct expression of our own self-confidence and sense of worth. The fact that someone has the power to tell us what to do, to approve our work, and even to fire us, forces us to face our own feelings of power or power-lessness in life.

When we accept a job, we agree to cede certain kinds of authority to whomever we report to. The problem is that sometimes we unconsciously cede too much authority, or the wrong kind of authority. We flash back to our childhoods, when we had to do everything our parents and teachers told us, and when the consequences of disobeying were pretty dire. We forget that we and our bosses and underlings are all grownups with grownup abilities and lives.

When we find ourselves resenting our bosses—for whatever reason—our own unconscious, unresolved feelings about authority are probably involved. If we examine these feelings, our resentment lessens and we gain a clearer understanding of the situation.

Knowing where we stand with authority in our jobs helps us connect with our *inner* authority, our own inherent, unim-peachable power as spiritual beings. This inner authority is what guides us along our spiritual path; it's what helps us know the truth when we hear it. Our inner authority, further-more, is *always* within us, but we need to go through a spiritual growing-up process where we learn to listen for its voice, heed it, and trust it.

The more we connect with our inner authority, the more we see outer authority for what it is: a necessary aspect of human endeavor, something we agree to accept of our own free will. We also learn how and when to challenge outer authority, to go with our own gut instead of blindly following orders.

Burnout (Chapter 13). A potent mix of exhaustion and utter joylessness. That's why it's so insidious: You need some amount of joy to function, and once you've depleted your reserve, it's very difficult to build it back up. Think about this the next time you knowingly work too hard: You're not only pushing your body past its limit, you're also killing your own precious joy.

Imagine a far-off, magical land where every working person takes at least four weeks of vacation time (and often five or six), where lunches are relaxed, civilized affairs, and where burning out at one's job is *not* considered a virtue. Close your eyes. Can you see this astonishing place? It's called . . . *France*. Not a Utopia, mind you, just one of a goodly number of countries in the world where people don't habitually push themselves until they drop.

I'm not here to discuss the relative productivity of the world's industrialized nations. I just want to remind you that we have an unusually punishing work ethic here in the United States, begun by the Puritans and maintained by successive generations of striving immigrants. We take a perverse pride in working long hours and never using up our vacation days. Even if you don't personally subscribe to this work ethic, it permeates our culture and you can't help being affected by it.

All of which leads up to what I'm really trying to tell you: *Nobody's going to stop you from burning out in your job.* If you push yourself past the edge of exhaustion—and only you know where that edge is—you'll crash and burn. Not because your life is demanding, and of course it's demanding, but because you've ignored the frantic warning signals issued by your own body and soul. *Only you can heed those signals and give yourself the rest you need.*

Many times in your career, you'll find yourself in work situations that can burn you out if you're not careful. These situations are instructive: They teach you your limits. They show you the measure of your own endurance. They force you to ask yourself important questions like, "What am I trying to prove by working so hard?" Ideally, these situations force you to seek a truer balance between work and rest, between doing and being.

Change (Chapter 10). No matter what you hate about your current job, it will pass. Unfortunately, so will the stuff you love about your job. Get used to it. Good times and bad times tend to come in waves, and it's much better to ride those waves than to struggle against them.

Bad bosses replace good bosses, and vice versa, as inevitably as August follows July. Great staffs are painstakingly built, then recklessly dismantled. Happy work environments become miserable, then happy again. Job markets tighten and loosen like a yo-yo dieter's jeans. And the economy—I'm sure you don't need me to tell you about the economy.

The annoying truth is that you learn as much from the bad times as from the good times. Maybe more. A bad boss can be one of your most important teachers, especially if he/she teaches you to stand up for your own worth. Being laid off, or even being fired, can show you how strong and resilient you really are. Every painful experience in your working life can be a catalyst for spiritual growth, provided you're willing to take a good, hard look at the lesson it's trying to teach you—not in a spirit of self-flagellation, but in a spirit of trust that it's something you need, even want, to learn.

Besides, as I said, everything passes, including the good stuff. So if you love your job, love your boss, and even love your paycheck, enjoy this moment with abandon. The joyful times in your career, too, are great teachers. There's nothing like knowing what makes you happy in a job to teach you what sort of person you want to be, and where you want to go next.

Whether you're in an up cycle or a down cycle at the moment, the same general advice applies: Be wherever you are, feel whatever you're feeling, and then let it go.

Compassion (Chapter 16). A core spiritual value—and the most difficult value to preserve in a business environment.

Compassion is the ability to sympathize with another being's suffering, and the desire to alleviate that suffering. Compassion releases us from the tyranny of our own little egos. It teaches us that our own troubles, however great they are, are not the only troubles on Earth, that we are here to care about each other and care *for* each other. Compassion helps us experience other creatures' valor and nobility of soul. It helps us grow in love.

Compassion is also one of the first things we're encouraged to ditch in the business world. Business is a numbers game, seemingly a zero-sum game: You either make a profit or post a loss; you either win or lose, and if you lose, someone else wins. There seems to be no room for soft-heartedness when your very livelihood is at stake. If staff has to be cut during a recession in order for the firm to survive, well, the cuts need to be made and those people will just have to scramble for work. If a smaller firm gets squashed by a larger firm in the never-ending quest for greater profitability, well, that's just how it is. It's business.

Listen closely when you hear yourself say "It's business." Those words are usually spoken in defense of behavior that protects a company's bottom line at the expense of individual human beings. They represent a hardening of the heart. In business, decisions are made that cause people to suffer. Some of these decisions are more justifiable than others, but they are a fact of business life. When we steel ourselves and say, "It's business," we're really saying, "There's no place for personal feelings here." Or even: "I don't want to feel this. It's too painful." If we say these things to ourselves often enough, we run the risk of deadening our capacity to feel.

The challenge is to conduct business with our compassion intact. We may not be able to change the harsh realities of the marketplace, but we *can* allow ourselves to experience our own reactions to those realities. We can feel our fear of losing our jobs, our frustration at our own powerlessness. We can have compassion for the suffering of others, even if there's not much we can do to alleviate that suffering. We can observe our own failures of compassion, and learn from them.

Distraction (Chapter 14). A form of resistance to the task at hand; the state where your consciousness leaps about wildly and refuses to stay focused on one thing. Meditation teachers sometimes call this "monkey mind"—and, as I'm sure you know, monkeys are pretty smart creatures. Entertaining, too. There's nothing quite so fascinating as watching your own train of thought when it's bent on distracting you from the work you're supposed to be doing.

Do not assume that distraction is a negative thing. One of the most important aspects of meditation, in fact, is learning to observe your own distractedness—to watch your attention wander and gently bring it back to the task in front of you. Sometimes you accomplish this by focusing on your own breathing, a task that sounds easy but is actually well-nigh impossible. If you've tried it, you know that observing even one complete breath from start to finish without thinking about anything else is quite an accomplishment.

Distraction becomes the path to a focused mind: You learn

to focus by pulling your attention back from a state of unfocused-ness time and again.

And this (pay attention! I'm making a point!) is why your day job really *is* a form of spiritual practice: It confronts you with all kinds of tasks you don't want to focus on, but which you *have* to focus on because you could get fired if you don't. Enforced attentiveness! Do you realize how much you'd have to pay a meditation teacher for that?

You can't eliminate distraction, but you can learn to use it creatively. If you find yourself in a mental or emotional rut at work—if, for example, you can't find the solution to a thorny problem, or you can't stop thinking about what a jerk your boss is—you can choose a distraction that stops your mind from going around in the same old vicious circles. Make a cup of coffee. Call your mother. Pay your credit-card bill. Send that monkey on a useful errand—or go out and buy it a banana.

Dreams (Chapter 8). That's you, kid: a dreamer. It doesn't matter *what* you used to want to be when you grew up. It matters that you dared to love something enough to dream of doing it. Even if you're now doing something completely, wildly different for a living, you still need the passion embodied in your old dreams.

When you dream your childhood and adolescent dreams, you're forming an image of your best self, the self you'd like to be, the self you're trying to become. Of course, you know how dream language is—vivid, yet maddeningly indirect. If you dream as a child of wanting to become an astronaut, maybe you really *do* want to become an astronaut, whatever it takes. But maybe you're actually longing to escape the gravitational field of your upbringing in any one of a thousand ways. The point is that your dream contains vital energy that can propel you along your life path, even if you're not sure what that path is.

There comes a point in many a life when childhood and adolescent dreams have to make way for adult realities. The problem is that when that time comes, we often jettison the dreams altogether. If we study something for love—music, poetry, art history—and can't make a living at it, we choose a more practical profession and let the musician/poet/art lover languish. This, I submit, is the reason for much of the joylessness in the average workplace: We bring the "practical" adult to the office and leave the childhood dreamer at home.

Well, dreams *are* practical: You can't create your life without them. You can't envision a better self, a better life, a better world, and make them a reality. Your dreams, realized or not, are the other half of your life, the numinous, creative half. They connect you with your own capacity for love. Don't shut the door on them. Honor them.

Enlightenment (Chapter 18). I've always thought "enlightenment" to be a pretty vague concept and dubious as an end in itself. On the one hand, you're seeking a new level of understanding, a greater vision, a revelation of divine reality. All good stuff. On the other hand, you're scrambling to escape your current unenlightened state, struggling to find a way out of whatever pit you've somehow dug for yourself. It has always seemed to me that people who actively pursue enlightenment seem very impatient to get there, and a bit ashamed about not having arrived there yet.

I suppose this has to do with our deeply ingrained sense of being "fallen" beings, our burden of sin (especially if we were raised in certain faiths that are big on sin), our knowledge of our own shortcomings. We may contain a spark of divinity, or more than a spark, but we also harbor ignoble thoughts, evil impulses, and more neuroses than I can catalog. We may be beings of light, but we're also, at least in part, frightened, self-centered children with plenty of growing up to do. The great temptation in seeking enlightenment is to reach frantically

toward the light to escape our own inner darkness. "Oh Lord,"
we pray, "Get us the hell out of here!"

Well, folks, "here" is where we happen to be, smack in the middle of light *and* darkness. If we really want to be enlightened—to see ourselves as we truly are—we need to know our divinity *and* our dark side. If we want to lead our own darkness into the light, we need to accept that darkness, not disavow it.

Here, in our light-and-shade reality, is where we encounter our imperfect selves and our imperfect lives, and are thereby made aware of the spiritual task before us. Here is where we get to acknowledge our own nobility for taking on such a task. Here is where we get to love life as it is and to love ourselves as we already are. When we "arrive" at enlightenment, here is where we'll be.

Enough (Chapter 3). Are they paying you enough? How much *is* enough, anyway? Enough to cover your basic expenses? Enough to put your kids through school? Enough to compensate you for having to show up at your office every blessed day whether you feel like it or not? Enough to make up for the dreams you jettisoned to take the steady paycheck?

Unless there's a trust fund in your life, you probably have to work to pay for your own necessities—food, shelter, medical expenses—and maybe a few luxuries besides. With any luck, you enjoy your job, at least sometimes. But as a gainfully employed person, you barter a good deal of your time and energy for a steady income, and there will inevitably be times when you ask yourself whether that income is worth it.

But that's not the real question. The real question is: How much is enough—for *me*? What do I really need to feel secure and fulfilled in life?

And: Am I enough? Am I sufficient in my own soul?

You are, of course. But sometimes it takes a long time, a long journey, to arrive at a sense of your own sufficiency. Earning your own money teaches you that you can take care of yourself, and that knowledge is invaluable. But the more money you earn, the more you tend to think you need. Eventually you reach a point where you realize that not even an enormous salary can compensate for a sense of inner emptiness.

Strangely, it's a good thing to reach the point where you feel empty inside, because that's when you can begin to let yourself be filled. That's when you discover that your own enormous soul is waiting to fill that emptiness—your own love; your own presence; the shape of your own life. Whether you call it God, Spirit, Now, or nothing in particular, its hallmark is an endless sufficiency. It's where the idea of "enough" begins and ends.

Focus (Chapter 14). How was your day? No, really: What, exactly, happened to you today, and how present were you for it? What were you thinking about on your way to work? Do you even remember the commute? What tasks did you accomplish? How did you feel while you were doing them? Quick: What did you have for breakfast?

Every New Year's Eve we wonder where the past year went, and marvel that it went by so fast. The older we are, the faster the years go by, until we start to panic that time may run out before we've properly lived our lives. The thing is, we *are* living our lives. We're just not present for them; we're not paying attention. At any given moment, our consciousness wanders off in a dozen directions (see **Distraction**), rendering us effectively absent from that moment. To feel fully alive, we need to observe our scattered, blurred consciousness and bring ourselves into focus.

Focus isn't something we're born with; it's something we learn. In meditation, we deliberately set out to focus on some object or other—a mantra, our own breath. But every moment of our lives offers an opportunity for focus. We can choose to be present, feel what we're feeling, experience what we're experiencing, or we can let our minds wander away from our bodies and emotions and live our lives in our customary fog. The fog is easier, but we lose ourselves in it. If we can at least notice the quality of the fog, we become less lost in it.

Sometimes we're lucky enough to be seized by a task and drawn into it. We enter the so-called "flow" state, where we're utterly absorbed in our work and absolutely present for what we're doing. In the flow state, the hours flash by, but we don't have that sense of having been absent from our lives. On the contrary: We've been hyper-present, hyper-focused. Flow states give us a feeling of connection to a greater reality, a feeling shared by artists and mystics. They take us out of time and into the present, the only moment there is. Flow states are gifts, glimpses of a life lived in total focus. Most of the time, though, it's just us, the fog, and our intermittent determination to see through it.

Good (Chapter 12). Oh what a loaded word this is. You want to be a good person, a good colleague, and a good worker, right? Well, yes. And being "good" is the same thing as being "spiritual," right? Well, no.

We want to see ourselves as dedicated, productive, capable workers who are also kind and caring colleagues. And we probably *are* all these things, to a degree. The problem is that we're probably also, to a degree, apathetic slackers who harbor

distinctly unloving impulses toward the people we work with.
We're both caring and uncaring, loving and unloving. And the whole mixed bag is "spiritual."

Many of us link the idea of striving to be good with the idea of striving *not* to be bad, and somehow we need to accomplish both ends in order to consider ourselves spiritually worthy. This is, to put it charitably, unworkable. We're spiritually worthy already, and our goodness (or badness) has nothing to do with it.

We strive to please our bosses and live up to our own idealized idea of good-worker-hood. Sometimes we push ourselves *too* hard because we're secretly afraid that if we don't, our evil twin will take over and we'll slack off entirely. We push ourselves to be good so we won't be bad. We've been doing this since we were about four years old, and it hasn't worked yet.

Sometimes we push ourselves to be good so we can feel superior to those around us, as though our merits had to be balanced by someone else's demerits, or vice versa. This is another concept we ought to have left in nursery school. You may think you *have* left it there, but believe me, it dies hard.

Our true goodness, I submit, lies in our willingness to see and accept every part of ourselves. Sometimes we're dedicated workers, and sometimes it's all we can do just to show up. The point is that we're never completely, perfectly good *or* completely, perfectly bad. We're just who we are. Every day we do the best we can, even if it's not so hot, is a good day.

Happiness (Chapter 9). In work, as in life, "happiness" is a term of art. We all talk about wanting to be happy in our jobs, but we don't all necessarily mean the same thing by it. We want a certain salary level, a certain amount of freedom or flexibility, a certain amount of recognition, a certain amount of joy in the work itself. We want to feel excited about going to work in the morning, or, failing that, not terrible about it. We want to feel we're doing something meaningful and useful with the zillion hours we put in over a lifetime. We want, in short, to feel good about ourselves in the context of our jobs.

The thing is, we don't give much active thought to the idea of vocational happiness unless we're not happy; we're generally much more conscious of the lack of happiness than of the thing itself. (When you have a backache, it's all you can think about; when it goes away, you don't dwell on your beautiful, ache-free back.) I'm betting that if I asked you right now to tell me three things that make you happy about your current job, you'd have to think for a minute. But if I asked you to tell me three things that make you unhappy, you'd rattle them off in a second: *My*

boss is a jerk. The hours are ridiculous. I don't have a window. 211
*My office mate is a total slacker. They've stopped serving
doughnuts on Fridays.* And so on. We know all about our various unfulfillments in life; fulfillment is harder to pin down.

Fortunately, our unfulfillments are important barometers in
our lives; they tell us what we need in order to become happy.
The things that make you uncomfortable about your job are
the things you need to work on—the issues you're ready,
though not necessarily willing, to tackle.

Viewing the things that make you unhappy as puzzles to
solve rather than crosses to bear gives you a sense of active par-
ticipation in your own life. Viewing your unfulfillment as a
path to fulfillment makes life seem a lot less bleak. Dealing
with thorny issues as they arise does not instantly resolve those
issues, but it does give you a feeling of accomplishment.
Which, by the way, makes you happy.

Love (Chapter 17). If you want your job to be a source of spiritual sustenance, you need to start treating it as though it
already were one. How? By bringing your whole self to your
job—including the part of you that loves. Love, after all, is
essential to your spiritual being. I happen to think it's the
beginning and end of everything.

It's love, after all, that connects us with others, with our own deepest selves, and with the divine. We work hard at maintaining our loving relationships because we know that love takes work, and we're willing to do that work to keep love flowing in our lives. So why not keep it flowing in *all* areas of our lives? Why not remind ourselves, at every possible minute, of our own capacity to love? Why not be truly subversive and love the people we work with?

Don't get me wrong. I'm not saying you have to *like* your colleagues. You don't have to pretend you care about them when you don't, and you certainly don't have to make yourself their personal patsy. But you can, perhaps, cultivate a little empathy for them, which is a doorway to love. You can try to see them as people who are in your life for a reason, people who might possibly be able to teach you something. It begins with a click of consciousness, a flash of compassion, a nanosecond's realization that your colleagues, too, are on a spiritual path; that they, too, are struggling for understanding; that they, too, are worthy of love. You may never feel that much love for them. But the whole experience of your job will change if you *consider the possibility* of loving them.

Giving love is the same thing as receiving love. I mean that literally. When you feel unconditional love for another being, you feel utterly fulfilled by it, even if only for a moment. When you love, you feel *loved*. It's a miraculous feeling; it's also your birthright. Why not bring it into every part of your life?

Perfectionism (Chapter 15). A trait many people are proud of, which actually brings them—and everyone around them—endless anguish. Whenever you hear someone say, "I'm a perfectionist," be prepared to deal with someone who regularly beats up on herself (or himself) and is probably just as prepared to beat up on you.

Perfectionism paralyzes you. Any task that has to be done perfectly becomes a task that can make or break you. Your whole identity is somehow riding on it, and you can't let yourself screw up—so of course, you take no pleasure in the task and derive no satisfaction from the result. A task that can be done imperfectly, by contrast, is a task you can have fun with, a task you can throw all your creativity at just to see what sticks.

Perfectionism is a habit we acquire very early in life. As small children, we try to be perfectly good to ensure a constant flow of our parents' love. This doesn't usually work out, because we can't be perfect children any more than our parents can be perfectly loving. But we still believe, and the belief dies hard, that we can maintain some control over our lives if we can only live up to our impossible standards of perfection. We become the voice in our own ear that says, "You can't blow this. Be careful . . . oh no! . . . you're gonna *blow* it!" I don't know about you, but when I hear that voice, I usually blow it.

Sometimes, by the way, we try to be perfectly *bad*—we decide that all authority sucks and we're just not going to abide by it. This is another attempt to control the world around us, another form of perfectionism, and it, too, is no picnic for anyone involved.

One of the joys of living in a deeply imperfect world is that we get to screw up in the process of learning to become our true, grownup selves. Screwing up, in fact, is the *only* way to learn. You can't get something really right until you've experienced the various ways of getting it wrong. And you can't truly excel at a task until you let yourself relax into it, until you let go of your controlling perfectionism and remember what it feels like to *play*.

Practice (Chapter 1). Are we there yet? Nope. Any musician will tell you that practice never ends. Once you've nailed the technical demands of a piece, your work is just beginning. You still have to find a way to communicate the composer's heart, soul, and intellect via those little black notes on the page; not to mention your *own* heart, soul, and intellect. Practice in music often means playing the same phrase over and over, thinking about the same few measures over and over, making the same mistakes over and over.

However: The ultimate object of practice is to forget everything you've practiced and just *play*—to let the music speak through you in the moment, aided by the technique you've so painstakingly acquired. If, as Einstein said, chance favors the prepared mind, then music favors the prepared performer.

Spiritual practice is not all that different from musical practice. In meditation, for example, you attempt to learn focus, concentration, and mindfulness by trying over and over (and often failing) to achieve them. You know you're going to zone out, let your mind wander, or hitch a ride on your own free-floating anxieties. You also know you're building a technique for spiritual awareness—quieting your mind, preparing your soul for whatever comes. Sometimes wonderful things come. Sometimes the divine speaks in you. Sometimes not. After a while, you realize that getting there isn't really the point. Being here is the point: being whoever you are right now, and giving it your best shot. Even if you're a great musician or a Zen master, it still comes down to this moment and you in it, doing the very best you can.

At your job, you also find yourself facing the same challenges and frustrations over and over. I'm not just talking about mastering new skills, but about relating to your co-workers, dealing with authority issues, and generally feeling good about the hours you put in every week. If you face these challenges and frustrations mindfully, with compassion for your own struggle, you gradually begin to master them. More important, you begin to cut yourself some slack: You begin to treat your workday life as an active part of your spiritual practice, where challenges, frustrations, and imperfections are the very things you're here to work on.

Prayer (Chapter 7). Literally, a request, an entreaty. But who's entreating whom, and for what?

For starters, you're asking yourself to be present: to stop what you're doing and center yourself, to gather your consciousness about you, conflicts, messy emotions, and all. You're also asking that the divine be present for you and that you be present for the divine, right here, right now. Anytime you wake up in the moment and register your own presence, you're praying. "Here I am" is a prayer.

If you're not sure where you stand with the idea of divinity, you can at least open yourself to the possibility that some larger reality exists and you can experience it empirically. That larger reality—God, your own divinity, spirit, prana, the Tao, whatever you call it, however you experience it—can be found only in the present moment, through your presence in it. This is why the mere act of showing up is so enormously important.

You know how sometimes you have to remind yourself to breathe deeply—to fill your lungs, expand your abdomen, take fresh air in and push the old, stale air out? Of course, breathing is involuntary; you'll do it whether you're thinking about it or not. But a deep breath, taken in full awareness, is very different from a shallow, tight-chested breath. It brings your entire body into the act; it gives you strength to run, or lift a weight, or sing, or speak in an authoritative voice. It brings *you* into your body.

Prayer is like that deep, conscious breath. You are inherently a divine being whether you're aware of it or not, but prayer connects you to that larger, divine self. It connects you to a source of wisdom and strength and keeps that connection open.

If you don't know how to pray, just shut up. Build the silence, and prayer will come.

Relationship (Chapter 9). *It's the people, stupid!* Human relationships are the real stuff our careers are made of. It's the people we work with who make our jobs wonderful or awful, not the title, salary, or the prestige. Look back on the best job you've had so far. I'm willing to bet you had a great boss, or a great group of colleagues, or both.

Granted, there are all sorts of things that can make you miserable in a job. Maybe you're not getting the recognition you deserve; maybe you're overworked or bored to tears. But if you look closely, you can usually discover some human factor in your discontent. Maybe you don't let your colleagues know who you really are because you're unable or unwilling to express your true abilities or feelings. Maybe you choose not to relate to the people around you because you don't feel you belong in this job. My point is that if you feel uncomfortable around your colleagues, it's probably a familiar discomfort, one you've felt at some point in your past. Your life circumstances may change, but your relationship issues keep following you around until you face them.

Fortunately, your job provides an ideal laboratory for dealing with these unresolved issues. Which is a lofty way of saying that you tend to get thrown together with people who make you crazy, and those are the relationships that teach you the most about yourself. Is there, for example, a colleague you don't get along with? The friction between you can tell you something important about what pushes your buttons, and why. You may not be able to solve all the problems between you—you're in an office, not group therapy, thank goodness—but you can at least observe what sets you off, and how you deal with your own anger.

And the good relationships? You never forget them. They feed your soul.

Resistance (Chapter 2). There is no work without resistance, and I mean that literally. In physics, "work" is defined as force moving against resistance to produce motion in a body. If we try to carry an object, say, a grand piano, up a flight of stairs, we're moving it against gravity (among other things). The bigger the object, the greater the resistance, and the harder the work. This goes for spiritual work, too: The bigger the task, the harder you fight it. The problem you least want to face may be the most important problem you have.

You'll have noticed, I'm sure, that there are mornings when you don't exactly leap out of bed flushed with eagerness to get to your office and dive into the day's work. There may be tasks you need to do for very good reasons (e.g., you'll get fired if you don't do them), which you nevertheless resist mightily. Being a working person involves, to some degree, being in a chronic state of resistance to some aspect of your job. The fact that you have to struggle against this resistance does not necessarily mean you're in the wrong job; it just means you're human.

Don't hate me for saying this (okay, hate me if it makes you feel better), but resistance can be your friend, or at least your teacher. If you notice that you're resisting a specific task and observe what form your resistance takes, you're waking yourself up—becoming aware of who you are in the present moment. It's one thing, for example, to unconsciously put off writing a report because you hate writing reports. It's quite another thing to watch yourself procrastinating and ask yourself, objectively and dispassionately, "Why am I resisting this task? What, exactly, is stopping me?" In the first instance, you're prolonging your own agony. In the second, you're actively helping yourself approach the task—and showing yourself a little respect in the process.

Sanctuary (Chapter 11). We all need some kind of sanctuary in our lives, a space designated for the experience of holiness, whatever that means for us as individuals. A sanctuary is a place of refuge, a retreat from the relentless world, and it isn't necessarily an actual physical space. If there's a poem or a painting or a piece of music that comforts you and brings you home to yourself, that's a sanctuary.

If you're lucky, and I mean really lucky, your office will sometimes feel like a sanctuary: There will occasionally be a quality of space, silence, or light that will center you in the moment, remind you to breathe, call you to prayer. Don't count on it, though. Most office environments are about as far from sacred as you can get. They're noisy or oppressively lighted; they confront you with people and tasks you don't necessarily enjoy. And you don't choose to go there; in fact, you're stuck there. So how can you create any feeling of sacred space in your place of business, and furthermore, why should you?

Repeat after me, please: *My office is a sacred space by virtue of my own presence in it*. It may be the lousiest office in the building; it may not have a window, a door, or even proper walls. But for eight hours a day or more, it's occupied by you, a divine being on a spiritual path—whether or not you're feeling remotely spiritual at any given moment. Grappling with secular issues during the course of your workday is part of your spiritual practice. Experiencing your resistance to your job is part of your spiritual practice. Being gainfully employed is part of your spiritual practice. Be it ever so crummy, your office is a place where you bring your soul. Try to remember this once in a while.

Spirit (Chapter 1). I'm not going to presume to tell you what "spirit" is, for three good reasons: 1) Words can't describe it without flattening it; 2) It's intensely personal; and 3) You identify it not by what it is but by what it *does*, specifically, what it does to *you*.

You know how it feels when you slip on an invisible patch of ice and your feet fly out from under you? There's a moment of utter awareness: *Here I am, falling.* At that moment, everything else flies out of your head and you're simply there, falling. There's nothing else you can do but be there. An experience of spirit has that quality: It pulls you into a consciousness of the moment and your own presence in it. There's a sense of a greater, compelling force that simultaneously moves you and moves within you.

Spirit is the thing that calls to you and shakes you awake *right here, right now,* in the present moment. To be conscious of spirit requires your presence in this moment.

When you see the wind stirring in the trees and feel an echoing stir in your own heart, that's spirit. You recognize the enormity of creation, both outside of you and within you.

"The enormity of creation" sounds like one of those grand, abstract phrases, but it's actually very specific and practical. When you connect with spirit, you connect with your own creative potential—your ability to feel your own feelings, live your own life, walk your own path. You connect with your life as a work in progress, something that's shaped by you but also bigger than you.

Of course, the present moment—the place where spirit catches up with you—is accessible wherever you are, including your office. You are a spiritual being; wherever you are present, spirit is present. So even though it may seem oxymoronic to talk about finding spirituality in the average workplace, there's as much potential for spiritual experience at your job as there is anyplace else. All that is required is that you be present for it.

Vocation (Chapter 4). Literally, a calling. Remember that saying, "Many are called but few are chosen"? As far as I'm concerned, we're all called and we're all chosen. The trick is to recognize the call when we hear it—and to choose to listen to it.

If you've always burned to be a physician (or a pastry chef, or a pirate), you can't bear the thought of being anything else, and you're willing to do whatever it takes to get there, your

vocation is enviably clear. But if, like many of us, you've
reached adulthood without really knowing what you want to
be when you grow up, you're still being called. Your developing soul is calling you. It's trying to tell you who you are and
what you're here to accomplish. There are things your soul
needs to learn—greater compassion, perhaps, or greater confidence, or freedom from a certain kind of fear. There are shortcomings you need to acknowledge in order to become your
best self. One thing I can guarantee: Whatever it is you need to
learn, it's right in front of you. Your life situation, including
your job situation, is somehow bringing you face to face with
whatever you need for your spiritual growth.

Whenever you hear an inner voice saying, "I enjoy this
task," you're hearing your soul tell you something about who
you are. If you're good at filing, pay attention: Your gift for
order is sorely needed in the world. If you're a caring, effective
manager, you're blessed with empathy and clarity.

The tasks you hate are trying to tell you something, too. If
you hate sitting through meetings, for example, you'll find it
instructive to ask yourself why. Maybe you'd rather be out-
doors; maybe you don't want to feel like you're part of a
group; maybe there's some sort of power dynamic going on
that makes you furious. Whatever the case, exploring your

dislike will point you toward something your soul needs to
learn.

That's the deeper meaning of "vocation": Your own soul calling to you, and you choosing to pay attention to it in this moment, and the next, and the next.

Wallowing (Chapter 5). You might not expect to see this word in a glossary of spiritual terms, but believe me, it belongs here. Wallowing—dwelling on the negative aspects of the situation at hand—is the one surefire way to arrest your spiritual growth and prolong your soul's discontent. And for most of us humans, unfortunately, wallowing is as easy as falling off a log into a pool of quicksand.

The First Noble Truth of Buddhism is that suffering is an inescapable reality for all living beings. We suffer pain, illness, bereavement, and death, among other indignities, and there's no way around them. (Life's a bitch, in other words, and then we die.) What on Earth can possibly be noble about such a truth? Well, *we* can. We are noble, worthy of respect, because of the difficult tasks we undertake merely by being alive. We cannot experience the joy of loving someone, for example, without eventually experiencing the sorrow of losing that person; joy and sorrow usually show up in our lives as Siamese twins. Obviously, we try to hold on to our joy, even though joy is notoriously resistant to being held onto. Less obviously, we also try to hold on to our sorrow. We give ourselves extra points for suffering. In other words, we wallow. A certain amount of wallowing is human, but there comes a point where we need to move beyond it.

There's a surefire way to tell when you're wallowing in your own suffering: You hear the same tired refrain over and over, and it's some version of: I'm in pain and there's no way out. I'm in a dead-end job (and there's no way out). My boss is a bitch (and there's no way out). This company sucks (and there's no way out).

Well, you are in pain. But by wallowing, you're prolonging your pain indefinitely, and possibly encouraging others in your workplace to prolong their pain along with you. Wallowing begets more wallowing and very little else. The way out is to acknowledge the pain of the moment and then *let it go*. No matter how bad the situation, there is some tiny part of it that you can actually change for the better. Find that part and focus on it.

Work (Chapter 2). Everyone here who has a physical body, raise your hand. That's, let's see, all of us. So we all know what work is, because every physical action, voluntary or involuntary, requires some output of energy, and we all know what that feels like. In order to raise your hand, you need to contract the muscles that lift the physical weight of your arm, an operation that requires fuel, measured in calories. If you've eaten your Wheaties and stored that carbohydrate energy in your body, raising your hand is not a problem. In fact, you don't even have to think about it.

Do think about it for a minute, though. As physical beings, absolutely every action we take is a dance of energy. Muscles move, neurons fire. Cells metabolize their various fuels to power the chemistry of life. Electrons whirl madly and seemingly randomly about the nuclei of atoms. Energy is transformed from one state to another and back again. And in every one of these energy transactions, great or small, work is accomplished. Being in a physical body, living in a physical universe, is all about work.

As human beings, we have to tame our physical environment to survive—to create shelter for our furless bodies, to coax nourishment from the recalcitrant earth. Nowadays we're not (usually) building our own shelters and foraging for our own food, but we are putting in 50- or 60-hour workweeks to pay for whatever keeps us warm, dry, and fed. We take in energy, we expend energy, we create a life. This is our natural state. Physical effort—work—tires us out; but it also feels good. We need to feel we've accomplished something in order to feel truly alive.

The life of the spirit is just as dynamic as the life of the body, maybe more dynamic: We change, we grow, we transform ourselves. We take the stuff of our lives—mental, emotional, physical—and use it as fuel for our own growth. We strive to become better, freer, happier, more loving beings, and to give something of ourselves back to the world. This takes work, spiritual work—but, as I remind you one last, blessed time, work is what we're here for.